The Month of St. Joseph

St. Teresa of Avila reminds us of the Power of St. Joseph

The Month of St. Joseph

Exercises for Each Day of the Month of March

by the
Most Rev. M. de Langalerie, Archbishop of Auch

Translated from the French
by a Sister of St. Joseph
Permissu Superiorum

2014
ST. AUGUSTINE ACADEMY PRESS
LISLE, ILLINOIS

This book was originally published in 1874
by D. & J. Sadlier & Co.
This edition ©2014 by St. Augustine Academy Press.
All editing by Lisa Bergman.

ISBN: 978-1-936639-27-4

Contents

Eve of the First Day........................1

First Day
St. Joseph, Spouse of the Blessed Virgin.............9

Second Day
St. Joseph, Foster-father of Jesus Christ.............14

Third Day
St. Joseph, Model of Justice......................20

Fourth Day
St. Joseph, Model of the Life of Faith..............25

Fifth Day
St. Joseph, the Last and Greatest of the Patriarchs......30

Sixth Day
St. Joseph, Model of Remembrance of God.........36

Seventh Day
St. Joseph Confirmed in Grace....................42

vi

Eighth Day
St. Joseph, Model of Union with Jesus Christ 48

Ninth Day
St. Joseph, First Confessor of the New Law 53

Tenth Day
St. Joseph, Model of Hope 58

Eleventh Day
St. Joseph, Model of Patience and Mortification 64

Twelfth Day
St. Joseph, Model of Sufferings 70

Thirteenth Day
St. Joseph, Model of Ardent Charity 76

Fourteenth Day
St. Joseph, Head of the Holy Family 81

Fifteenth Day
St. Joseph, Model of the Hidden Life 86

Sixteenth Day
St. Joseph, Model of Justice 91

Seventeenth Day
St. Joseph, Model of Charity To our Neighbor 96

Eighteenth Day

St. Joseph, Model of Humility 101

Nineteenth Day

St. Joseph, Model of Religious 107

Twentieth Day

St. Joseph, Model of Obedience 113

Twenty-first Day

St. Joseph, Model of Religious Obedience 118

Twenty-second Day

St. Joseph, Depositary of the Secrets of God 122

Twenty-third Day

St. Joseph, Model of Prudence 127

Twenty-fourth Day

St. Joseph, Model of Chastity 132

Twenty-fifth Day

St. Joseph, Model of Purity .136

Twenty-sixth Day

St. Joseph, Model of Attention in Prayer 141

Twenty-seventh Day

St. Joseph, Model of Interior Recollection 146

Twenty-eighth Day
St. Joseph, Our Protector 151

Twenty-ninth Day
St. Joseph, Patron of a Happy Death 156

Thirtieth Day
St. Joseph, Patron of a Happy Death 162

Thirty-first Day
Benefits Derived from Devotion to St. Joseph 167

Act of Consecration to St. Joseph 170

Litany of St. Joseph 172

Prayer to St. Joseph 179

Novena to St. Joseph .181

Thirty Days' Prayer to St. Joseph 196

THE AUTHOR'S PREFACE

I N the preface of the "Introduction to a Devout Life," Saint Francis de Sales, anticipating the reproach of having devoted to that work more time than the care of a diocese could have allowed him, replied, with the great Saint Denis, that the perfecting of souls belongs principally to bishops, and their time could not be more usefully employed than in writing books the reading of which might animate souls to a desire of perfection. These words, even more than the success of the holy author of the "Devout Life," justify our own desire in the writing of this work. To have Saint

Joseph honored and imitated by the faithful, to propose to them the meditation of his virtues and the practice of devotion to him, appears to us an excellent means towards promoting the good of souls, in conformity with the desire of Saint Denis and the idea of Saint Francis de Sales. We are happy in the hope that even after our death this little work will inspire our brethren with holy sentiments, generous resolutions, love of God and of their neighbor. We recommend the spirit of sacrifice and the obligation which binds us to the practice of self-denial and Christian mortification. Each day we indicate a different means of bringing home to ourselves this important teaching of the Gospel; and the practices which we propose need not so engage us as to interfere with duties towards those claiming our attention. The great tendency of the age is a desire of comfort, ease, self-indulgence, and independence. Such being directly opposed to the spirit of Christianity, no effort should be spared in destroying it in ourselves and averting its dread consequences from others.

The Month of Saint Joseph occurs in Lent, during which season the duty of mortification of our passions and natural inclinations is more frequently recalled to our minds. The exercises of the Month of Saint Joseph must not conflict with those of Lent. We should assist at evening prayers in the Church, and attend to the particular instructions given there. These exercises in honor of Saint Joseph may form a supplement of devotion, which will be the more meritorious and profitable to our souls inasmuch as we will be the more exact in the fulfilment of the important duties imposed on us by the Church during the holy season of Lent. Nothing can replace the admirable practices of religious assemblies and the hearing of sermons and instructions taken from the gospel of the day, or the mysteries commemorated by the Church.

The duty of giving edification rests on each and every one of us. We should bear in mind that each parish is a family, the members of which are united by faith, and mutually owe good example to one another. Having opened by using his apology, so now we conclude in the words of our beloved Saint Francis de Sales: "A practised flower-girl so skilfully varies the hue and mixture that with the same flowers she arranges a great variety of bouquets; thus the Holy Ghost disposes with as much diversity the instruction of devotion, which is given us through the tongues and pens of his servants; that, although the doctrine be the same, the mode of treating it differs according to the several methods in which they are composed." Here is our bouquet, which, though much inferior to that of Saint Francis de Sales, we present with a heart deeply devoted to the salvation of souls.

Amen.

Month of
St. Joseph

Eve of the First Day

Ite ad Joseph.

Go to Joseph.

THESE words were addressed by Pharaoh to his subjects, who, when harassed by famine and distress, implored his aid. And we introduce them at the commencement of these pious exercises in order to establish a striking resemblance between the two patriarchs who, separated by an interval of seventeen centuries, have borne the glorious name of Joseph.

FIRST RESEMBLANCE: *The trials to which they were subjected.* Those of the first Joseph are so well known that there needs be no repetition of them. Pursued by the inveterate hatred of his brothers, and traitorously sold into slavery by them, he relied on God alone as the protector of his weakness and defender of his innocence. The second Joseph, though a descendant of the kings of Juda, lived in obscurity and poverty bordering on want. An outcast in Bethlehem, obliged to flee from Egypt, and abandoned by men, he was supported in his trials by his confidence, love, and fidelity towards God.

Let us learn from the example of these two great patriarchs how to endure the trials attendant on our journey through life, and let us be animated by the influence of this thought: God is with me, He loves and protects me. *Si Deus pro nobis, quis contra nos*—"If God is for us, who is against us?"

SECOND RESEMBLANCE: *The nature of their duties, and the manner in which these duties were fulfilled.* The first Joseph was a faithful servant in the house of Putiphar, a prudent and upright minister in the court of Pharaoh. Neither the allurements of pleasure, nor the fear of chastisements; nor the perfidious fascinations of human grandeur, could shake his fidelity. Ever faithful in his duty towards God, he was likewise dutiful to his master, occupying himself with the care of his own soul in preference to all other interests. The second Joseph was also a most faithful minister, in a royalty far more exalted and important than the one with which the well-beloved son of Jacob was honored. Charged by the Almighty, the Eternal King of ages, to be the protector of the life, and guardian of the virginal purity of the august Mary, Mother of God, he was likewise entrusted with the guardianship of the infancy and youth of the Saviour, thus bearing the relation of foster-father to the Redeemer of the human race.

My God! what a beautiful, grand, and sublime mystery! St. Joseph fulfilled his ministry agreeably to the wishes of his Sovereign, who himself deigns to render testimony to his justice when in the Gospel He says, "Joseph was a just man." But if Joseph was a just and, by consequence, a faithful and prudent guardian of the two inestimable treasures that were confided to him, it is because, as the Scriptures express it, "He hath not received his soul in vain." He knew that an account should be rendered of the manner in which he discharged his duty as protector of the virgin Mother and her divine Son.

Each one of us has a mission to fulfill, a ministry of some kind to exercise, and we should learn fidelity from the example of St. Joseph. Our eternal salvation depends on the faithful discharge of our duties. The saving of our own soul would be in itself a ministry, but, alas! how many other souls depend also on us ! We should, then, while endeavoring to save our own souls, do all in our power towards the saving of souls confided to our care, so that at death these sweet words may be addressed to us: "Well done, thou good and faithful servant; because thou hast been faithful over few things, I will set thee over many things: enter thou into the joy of thy Lord."

THIRD RESEMBLANCE: *Their connection with Jesus Christ.* The first Joseph, in his trials and afflictions, as well as in his triumphs, is regarded as one of the most striking images of Jesus Christ. It was not without a mysterious coincidence that Pharaoh gave him a name signifying 'saviour of the world.' Though the second Joseph did not himself bear the name 'Saviour of mankind,' he had the privilege of giving it to Him by whom alone it was merited. He was appointed protector of the person of Jesus, his guardian and foster-father. Jesus redeemed the world, and Joseph guarded and protected Jesus. We have said that he acquitted himself as a just man and faithful servant in his great and elevated mission; but we must add here, that it was through the intimate and direct influence of the Saviour that he accomplished the designs of God, and arrived at the perfection of his ministry. He was one of the first and most admirable imitators of the great Model, whom he closely contemplated. The spirit of the Saviour became his spirit, whereby he attained that new birth mentioned by

Nicodemus, which consists of divesting ourselves of our own will, combatting our inclinations, and subjecting our passions to reason and religion, that our lives may be in accordance with the Spirit of Jesus Christ. The first Joseph felt this influence in an indirect manner, as all the just of the Old Testament participated in the grace of the Redemption, though in a way constrained by the fact that the institutions of the old law were not in themselves perfect. Dating from St. John the Baptist, the Blessed Virgin, and St. Joseph, the spirit of the new law spreads itself with a plenitude and rapidity which manifests the presence of the Incarnate Word.

Have we entered into the spirit of Jesus Christ by our fidelity to His law and conformity with His divine will ?

Ite ad Joseph: Come, then, to Joseph. God, the Sovereign Master, invites you to Joseph in confiding the Author of grace to his care.

Ite ad Joseph: "Come to Joseph," says the Holy Church; and it is not with her as of old with ungrateful Egypt, who, after a few centuries, had forgotten the memory of her benefactor. The Church, on the contrary, attaches itself by a closer tie to the remembrance of St. Joseph according as it recedes from the period of his mortal life. Instead of the material food with which the ancient patriarch fed the Egyptians, Joseph has received and guarded for us the life-giving bread descended from heaven to nourish and sanctify our souls. Like Jesus and Mary, you must repair the impious outrages and blasphemies against the majesty of God. Where is the virginal purity of Mary, where the glory of St. Joseph, when Jesus is spoken of by infidels as an ordinary man, and His birth not regarded as a miracle of the power of God? *Ite ad Joseph*. The first Joseph demanded the Egyptians to sacrifice and abandon their individual fortunes for the common good; and our Joseph asks you to divest yourself of your imperfections, to replace which he offers you the love of Jesus.

PRAYER

HOLY St. Joseph! behold at your feet humble clients, ardently desiring to profit by the graces attached to your example and intercession. We pray that during this month our souls may be prepared for the worthy reception of our divine Saviour. Guardian of Jesus! be our protector and our guide. Pray for us, and present our prayers, purified by thine, to the heart of Jesus and the immaculate heart of Mary. Amen.

RESOLUTIONS

DURING the course of the day recall to your mind the preceding reflections.

Repeat from time to time the invocation: "*Go to Joseph.*"

Enter into the spirit of the holy season of Lent, and comply with the requirements of the Church.

Do not seek dispensation from the Lenten fast without sufficient cause.

Recite the *Our Father* and *Hail Mary* once, and *St. Joseph, pray for us*, three times.

First Day

ST. JOSEPH, SPOUSE OF THE BLESSED VIRGIN

※

Sancte Joseph in Sponsum Mariæ pro omnibus electe, ora pro nobis.

Saint Joseph, chosen from among men to be the Spouse of Mary, pray for us.

FIRST POINT: The first and most essential attribute of St. Joseph is that of Spouse of the Blessed Virgin Mary. He is only the foster-father of Jesus Christ, but he is the spouse of the Virgin Mother of God. He was chosen from among thousands, from among tens of thousands, from among all men, to be honored by this glorious privilege. A pious tradition relates that when the choice of a husband was imposed on the Blessed Virgin, her guardian called together all her relations of the race of David and tribe of Juda. Joseph came among the others who aspired to the honor; but his modesty kept him at a distance until the Almighty, by a miracle, decided in his favor. Each candidate left an almond-tree rod in the temple in the evening, and the next day the dry and withered branch of Joseph, like that which of old secured the priesthood to Aaron, was found green and blossomed with fragrant flowers—graceful symbols of the virtues that had fixed the choice of God on Joseph to be the guardian of the most precious treasure, after the humanity of Jesus Christ, that earth ever possessed. That treasure belonged to God and to men, but in a particular manner to St. Joseph; for the sacred tie that bound the affections united the lives of Joseph and Mary. Let us admire this privilege, and congratulate our glorious protector on its possession.

Recall to mind the words he so frequently addressed to himself: Spouse of Mary; what an honor! what a grace! what a responsibility!

SECOND POINT: One practical reflection is the mainspring of the doctrine contained in the first point of this meditation. To Mary Joseph owed the honor of his close relationship to Jesus. He was regarded as the foster-father of Jesus only by his title of spouse of Mary, and the graces and privileges granted him were essential to his connections with her. This fact, important in its application to all Christians, is particularly so to us. Our relations with Jesus should be through Mary, since every good comes to us from Him through her. By His birth of her He became our brother, and we became her children by the adoption made at the foot of the cross on Calvary. Let us, then, go to Jesus through Mary, and to Mary through our glorious protector, St. Joseph. If we pray to him, he will obtain for us, by his intercession with Jesus and Mary, an abundance of heavenly graces emanating from the loving heart of Jesus and the maternal hands of our loving Mother, Mary.

THIRD POINT: What an honor! Let us repeat these words in unison with St. Joseph congratulating himself on the glorious title which united him to Mary. What an honor, what a responsibility, but also what a grace! These three words may be applied to all who have received vocations to leave all and follow Christ. Priests and religious should frequently entertain this salutary reflection: what a responsibility rests on those favored by God and honored with this grace of graces!

The Christian should ponder on these words, and apply them to himself. The vocation to Christianity by baptism is the greatest and most estimable of all graces. What an honor to be a child of God and of His Church, brother and co-heir of Jesus Christ, and the temple of the Holy Ghost! But, alas! what a responsibility to be the possessor of precious treasures carried in frail vases; for baptism has not freed us from the effects of concupiscence.

The fears awakened by this responsibility may, however, be removed by the thought of the superabundant graces which flow from the mercy and love of God—graces which are intended not only to be applied to our own souls, but which also are designed and should be made profitable to the many souls whose salvation and eternal happiness depend on us.

PRAYER

GLORIOUS St. Joseph, my holy protector, obtain that my soul may derive benefit from this first exercise. Thou who didst so often conduct Jesus in His infancy, guide me and protect me during these days which I offer and consecrate to thee. Lead me to Mary and to Jesus, and teach me to know and love them more fully and ardently.

RESOLUTIONS

DURING the course of the day recall to your mind the preceding reflections.

Repeat from time to time the invocation: *St. Joseph, spouse of the Blessed Virgin: Mary, pray for us.*

Jesus, Mary, and Joseph.

Restrain curiosity.

Accept, without ill-humor, the vexations consequent on the exercises of duty and charity.

Do not eat between meals.

Recite the *Our Father* and *Hail Mary* once, and *St. Joseph, pray for us*, three times.

Second Day

ST. JOSEPH, FOSTER-FATHER OF JESUS CHRIST

⚜

Sancte Joseph, cujus filius dici putari dignatus est filius Dei, ora pro nobis.

St. Joseph, foster-father of the Son of God, pray for us.

ST. JOSEPH is not, it is true, the father of Jesus Christ according to nature, nevertheless his office towards the Son of God gave him all the rights of paternity.

FIRST POINT: *God manifestly recognized the parental right of St. Joseph.* Previous to the advent of Christ, it was the design of Providence to conceal from the world and from Satan the coming of the Saviour and his birth of a virgin; hence God willed that St. Joseph should be regarded as the father of our Lord. To manifest this design, all the rights and all the honors of paternity were accorded to him, and his heart was animated with parental love towards Jesus. As the gifts of God are never recalled, it follows that during all eternity St. Joseph will possess these privileges. Sweet and cherished thought for hearts devoted to the service of God! Solid and immovable foundation on which to raise a tender and ardent affection to St. Joseph! These thoughts are evidently and clearly established, since Heaven has deigned to confirm, by a singular development, the extent of the glory of St. Joseph. Let our mind dwell on these three truths: God has given to St. Joseph, *first*, The honor of paternity towards our Lord; *second*, The rights of this paternity; *third*, Most paternal affection for him. What precious gifts, rich in the wealth of power implied in their possession! What treasures of tenderness and bounty they place in the heart of St. Joseph!

SECOND POINT: *St. Joseph's right of paternity is recognized by men.* That St. Joseph, during his life, was regarded as the foster-father of our divine Saviour is proved by the language of the

Jews on various occasions. Is He not, say they, the son of Joseph, the son of the carpenter? These were, according to their idea, expressions of contempt for our Lord ; they knew not that these words served to increase beyond measure the dignity and standing of His foster-father. They would have known this, had the mystery of the Incarnation been revealed to them as it was to St. Joseph. But as their hearts were not prepared for this favor, the knowledge was not accorded them. St. Joseph held secret this revelation by the command of God. He loved this silence, inasmuch as it was to him a source of happiness to obey the God of mercy and truth. His title of father was universally recognized by his contemporaries; and he regarded it as an incomparable honor to be associated in this most intimate manner with the ignominies of the Saviour. Of Jesus Christ they said: "This is the son of the carpenter;" of St. Joseph they might have said: "This is the father of the Galilean." Let us learn from this example that, when the wicked inflict outrages and persecutions on us, they serve to promote our honor and glory, providing we suffer them for God or in the cause of religion. We should rejoice to be deemed worthy of persecution for justice's sake. Let us pardon our persecutors, and love them, that our patience may triumph over their malice, and redound to the eternal honor of the Christian faith. *Vinco in bono malum*— "Overcome evil by good."

THIRD POINT: *St. Joseph's right of paternity manifested by the actions of our Lord.* "He was subject to them." This one sentence of the Gospel suffices to show that our Lord was subject to Joseph and to Mary as a son is subject to his parents. Jesus was regarded as the son of Joseph, as much by the respect, deference, and affection which he manifested toward his foster-father, as by all the other appearances which justify this title. And Jesus would not act a part. It was necessary that He should experience—let us speak clearly—that He should really feel for St. Joseph the sentiments which were expressed in His manner towards him. Jesus Christ, then, had for St. Joseph the heartfelt affection of the most tender, loving, respectful, and obedient of all sons. Let us congratulate St. Joseph on this filial tenderness which our Lord had for him. How many spiritual favors must have been given St. Joseph, and what an increase of virtue and merit must have been produced in him by the love of Jesus! A proof is hereby given us of the powerful protection of this great saint. Were I master, what would I not do for my parents? said a good son. Jesus Christ is Master, and during life He gave His foster-father virtue, which is more than all the riches and treasures of the earth; and now, in heaven, He gives him power.

PRAYER

HOLY St. Joseph, foster-father of Jesus Christ, behold at your feet His brethren and your children. Have for us the solicitude of a father. Take from us the joys of home, family, and country, if their possession be detrimental to our souls; seek for us if we wander from the path traced out by your example; seek us until we will have heard your voice; receive our petitions; dry our tears; guard us, and grant that we may always be to you as was the divine Saviour Himself— tender, submissive, and respectful. Amen.

RESOLUTIONS

DURING the course of the day recall to mind the preceding reflections.

Repeat occasionally the invocation: *St. Joseph, foster-father of Jesus Christ, pray for us.*

Refrain from light reading.

Endure cheerfully the inclemencies of the season.

Recite the *Our Father* and *Hail Mary* once, and *St. Joseph, pray for us*, three times.

St. Joseph, Model of Justice

✥

*Sancte Joseph, qui in Evangelio vocatus est justus,
ora pro nobis.*

St. Joseph, who in the Gospel is styled just,
pray for us.

FIRST POINT: *St. Joseph was just.*

Every Christian should strive to merit the attribute of justice. It is not sufficient for him to possess honesty and uprightness. An honest man may be guided solely by the uncertain light of reason; and he may be governed by a conscience which is perhaps influenced by public opinion. The just man, on the contrary, is directed by the word of God and by the will of God, as clearly demonstrated in the Church, and he relies on the assistance of grace for the accomplishment of the Divine will in himself. He says with David, "Make me to understand the way of Thy justification, and I shall be exercised in Thy wondrous works. I have run in the way of Thy commandments, and Thou didst enlarge my heart." Beautiful words! the sense of which is a thousand times repeated by the prophet. St. Joseph must have pronounced them frequently, for they were ever in his heart. It was the law of God, the will of God, and the word of God, which served him as the rule, the principle, and the support of his life and actions. What is our principle, and what our rule of action? Let us not be content with gaining the esteem of men, and being considered honest according to the standard of public opinion. As Christians and children of God, we should regulate our conduct by the example of Jesus Christ and the will of the Eternal Father.

SECOND POINT: *St. Joseph was just.* Justice, in the language of the Holy Scriptures, embraces all virtues. By failing in one, we shall incur the displeasure of Him who inculcated them all; for as St. James says, "And whosoever shall keep the whole law, but offend in one point, is become guilty of all." St. Joseph was not governed by natural inclination nor self-interest. He was just—just always, in all things, and towards all persons. Can we render a like testimony of ourselves? Is there not some one virtue, the practice of which we entirely neglect? We frequently allege our natural bent of character as an excuse for the defects over which we should watch with the greatest care, on account of their having become to us a second nature. Alas! character and habit cause us to commit many faults, and retard us in the acquisition and practice of virtue.

THIRD POINT: *St. Joseph was just.* The word *justice* reminds us that we owe God the fulfillment of every virtue, and it is in this sense that the word is used by the writers of the sacred Scripture. To be just implies the possession of all virtues. God has an absolute right to our entire submission. He aids us by His grace in every act of supernatural virtue; hence our virtues and merits appertain much more to Him than to ourselves, on account of the powerful and indispensable assistance given us in the acquisition of them. St. Joseph, deeply impressed with these thoughts, was just and humble. We may say that he received innumerable graces, and was almost forced to respond to them; but every man is likewise given grace sufficient for his Justification. Let us, then, be just. God will demand a rigorous account of the talents He has given, or rather confided, to each one of us. Every soul should increase in virtue according to the measure of graces which it receives. God, who is infinite justice, eternal bounty, and everlasting love, will be guided in His judgments equally by justice and mercy.

PRAYER

ST. JOSEPH, intercede for us. Ten just souls would have sufficed to save the guilty city. These ten souls could not have presented an homage so acceptable to God as thou alone canst offer Him. Their supplications could not have moved the heart of Jesus as thine can awaken its compassion. Pray, then, for us, our kind protector, and save us from the Divine anger. Obtain for us grace to fulfil our duties, correct our faults, and practise virtue.

RESOLUTIONS

RECALL to mind the preceding reflections.

Repeat from time to time: *St. Joseph, Model of Justice, pray for us.*

Recite the *Our Father* and *Hail Mary* once, and *St. Joseph, pray for us*, three times.

Fourth Day

ST. JOSEPH, MODEL OF THE LIFE OF FAITH

✠

Sancte Joseph, qui in Evangelio vocatus est Justus, ora pro nobis.

St. Joseph, who in the Gospel is styled just, pray for us.

FAITH is the source, the rule, and the principle of the moral and spiritual life in the soul of the just man. His mind is impressed and occupied with the teachings and practices of faith. For the better understanding of this mysterious, all-ruling power, let us consider the life of faith in St. Joseph.

FIRST POINT: *Faith manifested in the life of St. Joseph.* St. Joseph submitted his understanding to the most profound mysteries of faith, even when these mysteries demanded the greatest sacrifices on his part. He believed that God spoke and manifested His will to him; hence his faith was reasonable. Our faith should be strong and lively, for it is eminently reasonable. We believe incomprehensible mysteries, it is true, but our belief is based on the word of God, for He speaks by means of enlightened prophets and incontestable miracles. Ancient proofs, some of which are renewed in our own days, attest that the Church is the divinely authorized interpreter between God and man. Faith adds to the light of reason by manifesting new objects of knowledge, and it confirms truths of the natural order by its unexceptionable testimony. If the human intellect would gain in strength and power, let it be penetrated by the life of faith. The greatest and sublimest intellects were believers.

SECOND POINT: *Life of faith in the heart of St. Joseph.* Faith assumes its true character and essential quality only in the heart of the believer. The damned believe and tremble. Their knowledge gives but remorse, and causes them to blaspheme the truths to which they are forced to testify. Such is not the faith of the just man; such was not the faith of St. Joseph. He revered the mysteries which were successively revealed to him, and he lived in the hope of the promised Redeemer, ardently desiring and awaiting His coming. Let us cherish our faith, and, above all, let the emotions of our heart be directed by its saving influence. Every mystery of our holy religion proves the bounty and love of God towards his creatures. Faith finds a subject for thanks and love even in the contemplation of hell, into which the devil would drag us, that there we might join with him blaspheming God. Is not the fear of hell one of the most effective means to preserve us from the severity of the judgments of God? Though here on earth we may faintly perceive the greatness of the love that God bears us, it is only in heaven that we shall fully understand its plenitude.

THIRD POINT: *Life of faith in the actions of St. Joseph.* In the various circumstances related in the Gospel concerning St. Joseph, we learn that he conducted himself according to the lights given him by God, and not merely to human wisdom and prudence. We are thereby authorized to conclude that in those actions not mentioned, St. Joseph was actuated by the same principle. He was a lover of justice, and he lived the life of faith. This life does not consist in the performance of great or singular actions, nor in certain religious practices, even though these practices should form a daily order of exercises. It is a series of acts ever active and always acting. Faith harmonizes the conduct and animates every work. It directs our thoughts and moderates and purifies our sentiments. It solicits the grace and blessing of God on our repasts; it invokes His paternal care over our repose and our relaxations, that they may exceed in nothing, and be conformed in all things to the Divine will. It supports, animates, and strengthens us in our labors and occupations, by teaching us to offer them to the majesty of God, or to honor His infinite bounty. It reminds us of heaven, and detaches us from earth, conformably to those words of St. Paul: "If you be risen with Christ, seek the things that are above, where Christ is sitting at the right hand of God; mind the things that are above, not the things that are on the earth."

PRAYER

MY God, I firmly believe all the sacred truths the Catholic Church believes and teaches, because Thou hast revealed them, who neither canst deceive nor be deceived.

RESOLUTIONS

DURING the course of the day, recall to mind the preceding reflections.

Repeat, from time to time, the invocation: *St. Joseph, model of the life of faith, pray for us.*

Conform your will to the will of God.

Say a decade of the Rosary for the souls in Purgatory.

Recite the *Our Father* and *Hail Mary* once, and *St. Joseph, pray for us*, three times.

Fifth Day

St. Joseph, the Last and Greatest of the Patriarchs

Sancte Joseph, patriarcharum culmen, ora pro nobis.

St. Joseph, the last and greatest of the patriarchs, pray for us.

FIRST POINT: *We find increased and perfected in St. Joseph that which we most admire in the patriarchs.* The authority of the patriarch extends itself to all, and rules all things with a sovereign independence. The patriarch is a figure of God ruling His children and servants. He commands with an absolute authority which is always respected. St. Joseph appears thus to us in the family of which he is the head. Let us follow him to Bethlehem, to Egypt, and to Nazareth, and see him everywhere supremely exercising his paternal authority. He acts in the name of God, and as His immediate representative. What family can be compared to this, wherein Jesus and Mary are members? What supereminent authority is implied in the power to command a God made man and His Mother, the most privileged of all creatures; and at the same time, what admirable sweetness do we behold in the exercise of that patriarchal authority in him who is to become the type of Christian paternity! Christian parents, in the government of your children, take for your model the patriarch St.Joseph. Learn from him to command according to the right you hold from God, and with the sweetness inspired by the example of St. Joseph. Thus you will gain the obedience, respect, and love of your children. At the same time, understand that, to possess the authority of the patriarchs, it is necessary to have their spirit.

SECOND POINT: *Consider the spirit of the patriarchs.* St. Paul says, "All these died according to faith, not having received the promises, but beholding them afar off, and saluting them, and confessing that they are pilgrims and strangers on the earth." The greatest among them lived only in tents. Behold the spirit of the patriarchs! The passing enjoyments and terrestrial happiness which God allowed them did not divert their minds from the final object—the bliss of heaven; though faith taught them this could not be obtained until after the death of the God-Man, and His triumphant ascension into heaven. This spirit was perfected in St. Joseph. It is true he did not wait as long as his predecessors had waited for the accomplishment of these promises. The time of his death almost coincided with the epoch long and ardently desired by the patriarchs, when their souls should arrive at the possession of heavenly delights purchased for them through the merits of Jesus Christ. "The days of my pilgrimage are few and evil," said Jacob, notwithstanding the many consolations with which divine Providence alleviated his sorrows. Tradition tells us that the days of St. Joseph were fewer and more sorrowful. But the thought of heaven, which was to be the recompense of his life of trials and sacrifice, assuaged his pains—that heaven of which the society of Jesus and Mary had already given him a foretaste; that heaven which he greeted as near, was to him a subject replete with desire, hope, and happiness.

Christian parents, such should be your spirit. We have not here a lasting city. Your children are given you more for the purpose of fitting them for heaven than of qualifying them for earthly positions. Possessing these thoughts and this spirit, a sense of your sublime duties will be imposed upon you, and impressed upon your children. Having the spirit of the patriarchs, you will possess their authority also, and thus perpetuate the patriarchal family.

THIRD POINT: *The numerous posterity of the patriarchs.* The patriarchs numbered their children by families, and, from the tribute given for each member, they knew the number of their subjects. God multiplied them so that in number they equalled the sands of the sea

or the stars of the firmament. The family of
St. Joseph is not less blessed in the prodigious
number of his posterity. His is the family of
Jesus and Mary—the Christian family. Who
can enumerate this family, propagating its
members everywhere, and with them their
traditions and their faith? In what is the
patriarchal family comparable to the children
of St. Joseph? Thank God for having called
you to be a member of this family, and prove
yourself worthy of the favor by maintaining
yourself and your associates in the spirit of Jesus
Christ. Strive to merit for yourself a plenitude
of the spiritual benedictions corresponding
to the fruitfulness of the patriarchal family.
Your counsels, authority, and example can
engender numerous children to God and to
the Church. How great is the posterity of the
saints, multiplied in the orders of which they
are the founders, in the sinners converted by
their teachings, and the saints formed by their
example, their writings, or their intercession!

PRAYER

GLORIOUS St. Joseph, whom I am happy to call father, since I belong to the family over which your patriarchal authority was exercised, obtain for me the grace to comply with my duties. In all my undertakings, obtain for me the spirit of detachment for created things, and a desire of heavenly gifts.

RESOLUTIONS

RECALL to mind the preceding reflections.

Repeat occasionally the invocation: *St. Joseph, the last and greatest of the patriarchs, pray for us.*

Restrain your desire to converse on useless subjects.

Mortify your sense of taste at dinner.

Recite the *Our Father* and *Hail Mary* once, and *St. Joseph, pray for us,* three times.

Sixth Day

St. Joseph, Model of Remembrance of the Presence of God

※

Sancte Joseph, patriarcharum culmen, ora pro nobis.

St. Joseph, the last and greatest of the patriarchs, pray for us.

FIRST POINT: The patriarchs had a lively and a constant remembrance of the presence of God. This was incident to the expectation and hope in their redemption by the Messiah whom God, in His boundless mercy, had promised them, and of which promise we have spoken in the preceding meditation. It was owing also to the frequent communications with which the Almighty deigned to favor them, either in dreams and illuminations, or by the ministry of angels. It was likewise due to the spirit of faith by which their love was animated. This remembrance of the Divine presence caused them to address Him with remarkable familiarity as the God of Abraham, of Isaac, and of Jacob. It was, at the same time, a powerful help to keep them in the practice of virtue, and make them advance in the perfect accomplishment of the Divine will. "Walk before me, and be perfect," said God Himself to Abraham. This attention to the presence of God is the ladder of perfection in every state and condition of life. St. Joseph, the last and greatest of the patriarchs, understood more clearly than did any other the excellence of this means of perfection, and he practised it more faithfully. To convince one's self of this truth, it suffices to consider that St. Joseph was more impressed with heavenly thoughts than the angels could have been; that he was favored with intimate communications from God more frequently than they were; and that his whole life was animated by faith. Other proofs are to be given, but, before we offer them, let us beg of God, through the intercession of St.

Joseph, that our minds may be penetrated with an habitual sense of His presence, particularly during prayer and before our principal actions.

SECOND POINT: Two things are necessary as a means whereby to acquire this remembrance of the presence of God in a direct and practical manner: *first*, To meditate on God and His perfections, and be impressed with the necessity and plenitude of His being; *second*, It is necessary to have these thoughts react on ourselves by considering that God, by His omniscience, knows fully and clearly the motives which animate our thoughts, words, and actions, and even the secret workings of our inmost soul. The mind and heart of St. Joseph, initiated as he was into the mysteries of the Incarnation and Redemption, must have been continually occupied with thoughts of God—His providence, His love for man, His omnipresence, and His other infinite attributes, all of which were revealed to him. Manual labor did not distract his mind from the study of these truths. It occupied his time without debasing or entirely engaging his soul; on the contrary, his occupations left him even more liberty of thought and leisure than the study of science, politics, or the agitations of public life could have allowed him. Mechanics, laborers, and servants—all who are occupied in manual labor—can be interiorly united to God with much greater facility than can those whom they, perhaps, envy on account of belonging to a higher rank in life. Why do we not more frequently meditate on God, His perfections, and His love? Why do we not regard Him as a father, presiding over our labors, encouraging us by His presence and promise of the reward assured to those who offer and perform their works with the intention of pleasing Him?

THIRD POINT: Joseph had not only the remembrance of the presence of God to occupy his thoughts and rule his life; he had God really present before his eyes in the person of Jesus Christ. "And I saw, and I gave testimony that this is the Son of God," says St. John in the beginning of his Gospel. St. Joseph was the first witness of this wonder, in order that to him might be applied what was of old said to Abraham: "I am the Almighty God; walk before me, and be perfect." This actual Divine presence was almost unknown to the patriarchs.

We Christians have reason to rejoice in the privilege of being enabled to study the life of Christ in the: Gospel, and in receiving Him in the Holy Eucharist. We may, at every instant, find consolation in this sweet and divine presence, in which is a treasure of grace and heavenly benediction. Do we imitate St. Joseph in this regard?

PRAYER

HOLY Joseph, had I lived with you, my heart could have been easily impressed with a sense of the presence of God by thy example. Obtain for me that my heart be animated by a lively faith, so that all things may speak to me of God and remind me of His presence.

RESOLUTIONS

DURING the course of the day, recall to mind the preceding reflections.

Repeat often the invocation: *St. Joseph, the last and greatest of the patriarchs, pray for us.*

Do not contradict others nor criticise their actions.

Submit your will to the will of others.

Mortify your sense of taste at supper.

Recite the *Our Father* and *Hail Mary* once, and *St. Joseph, pray for us*, three times.

St. Joseph Confirmed in Grace

🙰

*Sancte Joseph ineffabilibus benedictionibus dotate,
ora pro nobis.*

St. Joseph, confirmed in grace, pray for us.

FIRST POINT: *St. Joseph is the Israelite descendant of Abraham, Isaac, and Jacob.* All the blessings given to the first-born of the patriarchs were united in him; and they assumed a new character hitherto understood with difficulty by the holiest persons, and seldom known through experience. St. Joseph, in the obscurity of his humble life, was animated by the spirit of the new law which the example and teachings of St. John the Baptist were soon to preach to all Judea. The old law promised temporal prosperity and eternal felicity to the Israelites who would be faithful in its observance.

The joys of the other life were to them remote consequences attendant on the coming of the Redeemer. The reward of a hundredfold in the life to come, promised by Jesus Christ for the trials and sacrifices endured here for His sake, must have been without attraction previous to the teachings of Christianity, and until a practical knowledge had been obtained of the merits of a soul suffering in union with a crucified God, and leading a life most opposed to the yearnings of nature. St. Joseph was, after the Blessed Virgin Mary, the first to manifest in his life this transformation of the blessings of the old law. Circumcised in the flesh according to the Jewish rite, he was circumcised in heart in the new spirit. His share of family inheritance during his existence on earth was poverty, exile, persecution, and the beatitudes of the Gospel. Do we understand and appreciate the blessings of the new law of love? Have we tasted of the happiness purchased by them? Are we circumcised in heart so as to joyfully endure poverty and suffering, and find therein that holy, ineffable, hidden sweetness promised by the infallible word of Almighty God? Do we not, on the contrary, imagine that happiness unalloyed is experienced by those only who are possessed of riches and enjoy worldly pleasures, than which no spirit is more opposed to the spirit of the Gospel?

SECOND POINT: *St. Joseph was the son of David, the descendant of princely ancestors, to whom the throne of Juda had been promised as an eternal benediction.* He was nevertheless a workman, and lived in obscurity, without influence, and not receiving the honors attendant on rank, position, and fortune. But he possessed a noble heart, which placed him far above his humble condition; and, despising the grandeur of an earthly kingdom, he has for a home the heart of Jesus, which is the new favor and the true royalty promised to the Christian family, of which he is the most illustrious representative. The royal line of David seemed to have terminated in the person of Joseph; but, on the contrary, it reigns for ever through Joseph and Mary, ennobled and transformed by their connections with Jesus Christ. And do we, who belong to this royal family, comprehend and esteem this sublime elevation? Are our hearts animated by sentiments of noble, generous, royal greatness, even though in a humble and lowly condition, or do we desire the honors and privileges of those above us in worldly standing? If Providence has blessed us with riches and honors, do we not prize them too highly, forgetting that the love of Jesus should be the highest ambition of a soul created to the image of God?

THIRD POINT: *St. Joseph was the last just man under the old law, favored by God with dreams of prophetic import.* He was the first who enjoyed those intimate ecstatic revelations with which the saints were afterwards blessed. He derived an abundance of precious graces from his constant relations with Mary and with Jesus Christ, the source and giver of all graces, and the mediator between God and man. St. Joseph was not elated by these many mysterious favors. He faithfully co-operated with them, thus meriting an increase of grace. We Christians receive frequent communications from heaven. What use do we make of them? Our guardian angels watch over and obtain innumerable favors for us; the Holy Ghost, by his sanctifying and inexhaustible love, is in close union with a soul faithful to his inspirations; and the Sacraments, particularly the Holy Eucharist, place us in the most intimate relations with Jesus Christ.

Christians! recognize your dignity; live in correspondence with these precious, superabundant, and divine blessings.

PRAYER

GLORIOUS St. Joseph, obtain for us the grace to profit by these blessings in which we as Christians participate. We are of the priestly and royal race, and have received the most glorious privileges. But are we conscious of the favors bestowed on us, and do we esteem them according to their worth? Your greatness consisted in virtue. Obtain for us that we may not by a criminal abuse of grace render ourselves the more guilty in the sight of God.

RESOLUTIONS

DURING the course of the day recall to mind the preceding reflections.

Repeat from time to time the invocation: *St. Joseph, confirmed in grace, pray for us.*

Listen to others with attention and respect, and, if there is error in their words, excuse their intention.

Say frequently, "Thy will be done."

Fast one day this week in honor of St. Joseph.

Recite the *Our Father* and *Hail Mary* once, and *St. Joseph, pray for us*, three times.

Eighth Day

ST. JOSEPH, MODEL OF UNION WITH JESUS CHRIST

✠

Sancte Joseph ineffabilibus benedictionibus dotate,
ora pro nobis.

St. Joseph, confirmed in grace, pray for us.

FIRST POINT: *Union with Jesus Christ is the most perfect expression of faith, and at the same time is its characteristic principle.* Spiritual life receives its vitality from Jesus Christ, and is the more productive of virtue and abundant in good works according as the union of the soul with him becomes more intimate. "Without me you can do nothing," says our Saviour. Without the aid of grace man cannot entertain a good thought. St. Paul says: "And no man can say the Lord Jesus but by the Holy Ghost." Our Lord makes use of a familiar and striking comparison in order to make this text more clear to us. Speaking to His apostles, He says: "I am the vine, you are the branches; he that abideth in me and I in him, the same beareth much fruit; for without me you can do nothing." Thus Jesus Christ continuously communicates His graces to us. A father of the Church, using another comparison, says that union with God is to the soul what air is to the lungs; for as we could not live a natural life without those successive inhalations which at short intervals cause the beating of our hearts, neither can our souls live the life of grace unless they receive spiritual nourishment from Jesus Christ. Let us live so as to be able to say with St. Paul, "I live, now not I; but Christ liveth in me."

SECOND POINT: *All true Christians experience the mysterious effects of the supernatural life, although they are not always perceptible to us.* To experience these effects, it suffices that our souls be in a state of grace, and that we frequently invoke Jesus Christ, and offer our principal actions through Him to God the Father. The more frequently we think of Jesus Christ, the oftener we invoke

Him; the more we beg His grace, which inspires us to imitate His example and obey His precepts, the more shall the supernatural life be perfected in us. We should be most unhappy had we not these simple and easy means of advancing in virtue, acquiring merit, and increasing our reward. In our days all men aspire to freedom. The greatest liberty is that given us by Jesus Christ in uniting us with himself, and enabling us to live in a Christian manner; for this union frees us from the thraldom of the world, the flesh, and the devil. It gives us a mastery over our faults, our actions, and elevates us far above all that could debase or degrade our dignity as Christians.

THIRD POINT: *St. Joseph understood and practised this indispensable virtue of a Christian life.* This union with God was not unknown to the just men of the old law. The principle and nourishment of their virtues were drawn from a belief in the merits of a Redeemer, and consequently from their union with Him. But this mysterious union has taken a wondrous development since the coming of the Redeemer, and the perfect fulfilment of the prophecies which previously gave His history to the just men who were not to see Him. St. Joseph, with the Blessed Virgin, was the first to contemplate the model of all justice. He saw and praised Him, adored Him as his God, and loved Him as his son. Are our lives in unison with that of Jesus Christ? Let us repeat these words, imposed on us as a dogma: Nothing without Jesus; on the contrary, all things by Jesus, in Jesus, and with Jesus—*per ipsum, cum ipso, in ipsum*—by Him as mediator of grace; with Him, our model and our strength; in Him, the sole object of the complacency of the Father.

PRAYER

HOLY St. Joseph, I dare not repeat the words of the apostle, "I live, now not I; but Christ liveth in me." Those words, which are the device of holy souls that love and practice union with Christ, I find impressed on your heart, and, perhaps, gathered from your lips. But, alas! I feel that I yet live in myself, in my own thoughts, in my predominant faults, in the love of riches, and in the susceptibilities of my nature. Help me, powerful saint, to live for Jesus, with Jesus, in Him, and by Him.

RESOLUTIONS

DURING the course of the day recall to mind the preceding reflections.

Repeat from time to time the invocation: *St. Joseph, enriched with graces, pray for us.*

Let your thoughts, words, and actions be in union with Jesus.

Conform your will to the will of God.

Rise promptly in the morning at a given hour.

Recite the *Our Father* and *Hail Mary* once, and *St. Joseph, pray for us*, three times.

Ninth Day

ST. JOSEPH, FIRST CONFESSOR OF THE NEW LAW

Sancte Joseph, legis novæ confessor prime,
ora pro nobis.

St. Joseph, first confessor of the new law,
pray for us.

FIRST POINT: The title given to St. Joseph at the beginning of this meditation might cause confusion in the minds of the faithful, unless fully explained. The holy Church gives him this title, and honors him in her public office as first among her confessors. We say that he was the first confessor of the new law, because he was the first just man who died under the empire and sweet influence of the law of love. In styling a great number of saints confessors, the Church does not mean to signify that they were priests and exercised the *ministry* of confessor, but it has adopted this manner of expression in the same sense that we would say to *confess* the faith, to *confess* the Gospel, or, more simply still, to *confess* Jesus Christ. Consequently, the word confessor should be well understood and sufficiently explained in the following point.

SECOND POINT: To confess Jesus Christ is to acknowledge and prove that we are His disciples; to believe all the truths, taught us by the Church in the name of Jesus Christ; and to practise His law as His ministers make it known to us. The resistance of the spirit against faith, and the flesh against the world and morality, exacts from the faithful a kind of martyrdom, and our confession derives its value from their interior violence and exterior combats. To confess Jesus Christ in a manner worthy the title of saint and confessor, is to believe the truths taught by the Church with a more lively and ardent faith than do the generality of the faithful; but especially to live according to the teaching of the Gospel with a devotion and perfection bordering on heroism. The holy confessor does not bind himself to follow the rigorous precepts of the Gospel, but he attaches himself to the observance of the counsels, and follows as closely as possible the divine Model, thus becoming in his turn an example to others. St. Joseph, then, confessed Jesus Christ in the manner indicated in this point of our meditation. He was the first after the Blessed Virgin to imitate Jesus Christ in a perfection until then unknown. He listened to Jesus Christ, and implicitly believed the truths received from the lips of eternal truth. He not only followed the rigorous precepts of the Gospel, but he moreover practised everything inculcated by the counsels, thus arriving at the heroic martyrdom of natural inclinations, and meriting the name of confessor. What simplicity yet incomprehensibility in the concise words made use of in the Gospel: *He was a just man!*

THIRD POINT: It remains now for us to examine and see if we confess Jesus Christ, His spirit, and His Gospel. We can enter heaven without being canonized saints and confessors, or without forcing on ourselves the fulfilment of the evangelical counsels; but it is not possible for us to attain eternal bliss if we do not, in some degree, imitate the saints and advance in the path of perfection. Not to advance is to recede. By a non-correspondence with the grace of God, we expose ourselves to lose our souls. St. Paul, addressing the faithful, says: "If you live according to the flesh, you shall die; but if by the spirit you mortify the deeds of the flesh, you shall live." Do our lives correspond with our profession of confessors of Christ and of His Church? Let us seriously examine our hearts, and correct in them what we may find opposed to the virtues of a true Christian. Let us thank God for having sustained us in the good we have accomplished, and humble ourselves for the non-conformity of our words and actions with our profession. May the words of our Saviour be applied to us: "Whosoever, therefore, shall confess me before men, I will also confess him before my Father, who is in heaven."

That is to say, I will, on judgment day, recognize before my Father, as my disciple, him who during life will have recognized me as his Master.

PRAYER

ADMIRABLE Saint! we have not up to this confessed Jesus Christ in spirit and in truth. Help us to correct all in our conduct, everything that is contradictory to our faith. Obtain for us the courage and strength necessary to fulfill our obligations as Christians and followers of Christ crucified. Grant that we receive all as coming from God, center our hopes in Him, and be faithful to His grace.

RESOLUTIONS

DURING the course of the day recall to your mind the preceding reflections.

Repeat from time to time: *St. Joseph, first confessor of the new law, pray for us.*

Do not question others through curiosity.

Let all your projects be subordinate to the will of God, and in all your undertakings depend on Him.

During meals attend to the wants of those at table with you.

Recite the *Our Father* and *Hail Mary* once, and *St. Joseph, pray for us*, three times.

Tenth Day

ST. JOSEPH, MODEL OF HOPE

❈

Sancte Joseph, legis novæ confessor prime,
ora pro nobis.

St. Joseph, first confessor of the new law,
pray for us.

FIRST POINT: Christian hope is a virtue which has for its first object future and eternal life—that is to say, the possession, knowledge, and love of God during all eternity—and for its second object the graces necessary as a means of attaining to this supreme end. Hence it leads us to believe that our past sins have been forgiven, and that God will raise us up and have pity on us if we should have the misfortune again to fall into them, though at the same time making us entertain the sentiment that God in His mercy will give us grace to guard against new falls. Moreover, it hopes and incessantly prays for the signal favor of final perseverance. How sweet are these thoughts, and how consoling this obligation of confidence in the beneficence of our Heavenly Father towards His children! Christianity alone makes hope a virtue, for it alone teaches us the opposite excesses of defiance and presumption. The unfortunate traitor Judas sinned against the virtue of hope by defiance and despair. To guard against presumption, we must rely on God alone, and distrust ourselves. Presumption caused St. Peter to deny his divine Master. Let us be penetrated with these thoughts, and dwell on them, and beg of God the virtue of hope through the intercession of St. Joseph, who practised it in its perfection.

SECOND POINT: The virtue of hope corresponds in a marvellous manner to the title of confessor, which, with the Church, we gave to St. Joseph in yesterday's meditation. To all bearing this title the Church applies this device of Christian hope. Happy is he who has not placed his hopes in the things of earth; and, indeed, this is one of the most precise lessons given us by Jesus Christ, and one that makes the difference between the old and the new law. The expectation of the Jews looked forward to transitory joys and terrestrial recompenses. Jesus Christ entirely effaced from His law this hope allowable to the just men of old. The mutable happiness of earth must be subservient to hope; and the true Christian will place no value on the joys of this life, since his proposed goal is eternal joy with God. The former teachings of Jesus Christ in the Beatitudes are the points of introduction to His doctrine. All the confessors of the new law must have understood the lessons and examples of Jesus Christ from this point of view, and St. Joseph was the first to receive and follow them. May the sentiments relative to Christian hope in this meditation affect our lives and actions, and tend to enkindle in our hearts the same degree of this virtue to which St. Joseph attained!

THIRD POINT: No earthly joys nor human consolations mingled in the hope of St. Joseph.

His future life on earth and in heaven was blended in the one same hope and love. Let us not view the condition in which Providence placed him as a preventive against the reverses of fortune. It was not to aid his great soul in the practice of humility that Joseph was poor and lived in poverty; but it was to teach us how our choice should be directed. Had he been rich, he would have sacrificed all and despised the worldly advantages of a brilliant future, in order to become more closely attached to the hopes of eternal life, to follow the example of our divine Master, and have impressed more deeply on his mind and heart the desire of eternal life. Or if, in obedience to the will of God, he had been obliged to live in prosperity, his whole life would have been characterized by voluntary self-denials, renunciation, and sacrifice. This is a salutary lesson, from which we must derive profit. We are not obliged to forego all pleasures and joys; but we should not allow our hearts to become attached to them, so that in the enjoyment of them we forget the desire of heaven. The more we seek for terrestrial happiness, the less we think of heaven; and the practice of hope, as taught in the first part of this meditation, would become impossible. *Sursum corda*—"Lift up our hearts."

PRAYER

HOLY St. Joseph! thy name is linked with hope. Obtain for me this gift, and let my soul be impressed with its sweet and amiable obligation of hoping all things from God. Grant that I may never more place confidence in human support, nor my happiness in perishable goods. Let the thought of the judgments of God only awaken a new cause for love. Teach me to live as a Christian, and to become worthy of the hope which your soul so fully appreciated. May I confide in God as the author of my salvation, hoping all things from His mercy, desiring to possess Him, the source of true joy, despising all earthly goods, guarding against them by continual sacrifice, and preparing my soul for the delights of heaven. Amen.

RESOLUTIONS

DURING the course of the day recall to mind the preceding reflections.

Repeat from time to time the invocation: *St. Joseph, first confessor of the new law, pray tor us.*

Address your inferiors attentively and politely.

Are not certain affections of our hearts too ardent and ill-regulated?

Observe mortification of the eyes.

Recite the *Our Father* and *Hail Mary* once, and *St. Joseph, pray for us,* three times.

St. Joseph, Model of Patience and Mortification

𝇈

Sancte Joseph, Christi patientis imitator prime,
ora pro nobis.

St. Joseph, first imitator of the sufferings of
Christ, pray for us.

FIRST POINT: The whole life of Jesus Christ was a cross and a martyrdom, says the author of the "Imitation of Christ." We may say that the life of a Christian must be the same. This conclusion is drawn from the Gospel. It resumes the teaching of the apostles, and proves that suffering is the chief characteristic in the lives of the saints. On this principle, and following these models, we must reflect on the necessity of sufferings. Coming from God, we must make them meritorious by a voluntary acceptance and loving offering, and sometimes even impose them on ourselves by generous acts of mortification and sacrifice. We have learned that the Christian must be a confessor by confessing Jesus Christ and Him crucified. These acts of mortification, directly opposed to nature, and painful to it, bear testimony of our love for Jesus. Thus the name of Christian may be regarded as synonymous with that of martyr. This is a severe but important lesson, one which, if understood and practised, would be an abridgment of all others, and which we seek, in the resolutions taken each day of this month, to implant in our souls, and to inculcate to others. St. Joseph is our model in this, inasmuch as we can apply to him in a true sense the beautiful and noble appellation of martyr.

Second Point: St. Joseph suffered in his senses, his mind, and his soul. First in his senses. He was a poor workman, and this occupation must have been painful to him, since he could number kings and chiefs of nations among his ancestors. The journey to Bethlehem, and the flight and sojourn in Egypt, were the cause of inexpressible suffering to him. Second, in his mind he endured painful apprehensions and motives of fear, less for himself than on account of those two precious beings who were placed in his charge, and whom he had to support and protect. Without imagining unknown perils, he knew enough of the Incarnation and Redemption to be convinced that the Saviour of the world would pay a great price for our ransom. His soul, as well as that of Mary, was pierced by the words of Simeon, and reflection often brought to his mind the mysteries in which he was an intimate participator. Thirdly, in his soul. There was no martyrdom more painful than the sufferings to which Almighty God was pleased to subject St. Joseph during the first periods of the Incarnation. God concealed the mystery from him, and made him witness of the condition of the Holy Virgin, his chaste spouse—a condition which seemed to accuse her of infidelity towards him and towards God. Mary, our holy and sweet Mother; Mary, the

Virgin Immaculate, must herself have suffered in the mental anguish of St. Joseph. Their reciprocal anxiety must have increased in one the suffering of the other. Add to this suffering that which was caused by the three days' loss of Jesus, and again the repulses met at Bethlehem, probably in Egypt, and at Nazareth. Moreover, in this detail of the sufferings of St. Joseph, we have mentioned only those coming directly from the hands of Providence; other voluntary sacrifices and self-imposed mortifications are the secrets of heaven.

THIRD POINT: We have explained the doctrine of self-denial, and given a great and touching example. Let us now compare our own conduct with this lesson and model. How far advanced are we in Christian mortification? Do we understand and practise its maxims, and do we comprehend its importance, its advantages, and its indispensable necessity, whether for the expiation of our sins, to prevent new relapses, or to advance in virtue—each act of which is naturally an effort or sacrifice—or to detach us from earth, and make the hope of heaven dearer and more precious to us—whether, in fine, to resemble Jesus Christ, who suffered so much for us, and thereby give Him the strongest proof of our tender affection? The thought of testifying our love for God, and manifesting our gratitude for His benefits to us, and our happiness in being allowed to endure pains and sacrifices for Him in commemoration of the sufferings, sacrifices, and affronts which he endured for us, should incessantly incite and animate us to bear patiently all the sufferings, pains, and sacrifices in life. But, alas! our most essential duties seem insupportable, for the manner in which we fulfill them indicates the repugnance we have for them. Let us be humbled at our weakness, and pray for more generosity.

PRAYER

GLORIOUS St. Joseph, thou wert a martyr in imitation of the Blessed Virgin, thy Spouse, and the Queen of martyrs. Thou, through prophetic revelation, hast been on

Calvary, and endured the lingering death of compassion, which in the Virgin Mother surpassed all the torments of martyrs. Mayest thou be blessed, our protector and father; for it was for us thou didst suffer! But thy soul, sustained by grace under the weight of its trials, was prepared by sufferings and voluntary sacrifices. Pray that I may be animated by thy example.

RESOLUTIONS

DURING the course of the day recall to mind the preceding reflections.

Repeat from time to time the invocation: *St. Joseph, first imitator of the sufferings of Jesus Christ, pray for us.*

Make choice of some sacrifices after the spirit of St. Joseph.

Recite the *Our Father* and *Hail Mary* once, and *St. Joseph, pray for us*, three times.

St. Joseph, Model of the Love of God and of Sufferings

✣

Sancte Joseph, in charitate ardentissime,
ora pro nobis.

St. Joseph, ardent lover of God, pray for us.

FIRST POINT: After the meditation made yesterday on the sufferings of St. Joseph, we must not imagine that our venerated and glorious protector had severe points of character, caused by sorrow and contracted by affliction. Calmness and mildness marked his whole demeanor, particularly his angelic countenance, and nevertheless he at all times suffered intensely. The mystery of this mildness, peace, and even joy, amidst sufferings, is explained by the influence of the love of God on the endurance of suffering and crosses, and the reciprocal influence of the love of sufferings and crosses on the development in us of the love of God. The love of God! These few words explain better than all others the great doctrine of the necessity of mortification and sufferings. Let us examine the subject of yesterday's meditation still more closely, and, placing ourselves at the foot of the cross, beg of St. Joseph that its sweet and precious influence may excite us to the love of suffering in union with Jesus.

SECOND POINT: When we truly love God, we feel ourselves drawn to the practice of mortification and to the love of sufferings.

First, because he counsels and commands them. He makes use of an express command, in which he places every one under the necessity of making sacrifices. "If any man will come after me, let him deny himself, take up his cross, and daily follow me." This is not simply an invitation, but a command, and one that is not addressed to a class of persons, but to all who desire to be Christians. We find in the Gospel several other maxims formal as this one, and numerous others which may be regarded as counsels; but counsels are sufficient for those who love. When love is sincere, it is easy to comply with the will of the beloved.

Second, God was the first to endure sufferings for love of us. We have already alluded to this motive, and would not again refer to it were it not so easy to repeat to ourselves, "Jesus Christ has loved me and delivered Himself to death for me." What a happiness for me to suffer for Him, like Simon the Cyrenean, who assisted Him in carrying His cross, and accompanied Him on His way to Calvary!

Third, God would not have advised nor commanded sufferings, nor would He have given us an example of love of sufferings, were they not to be in turn the strongest and truest proofs of our love towards Him. God is spiritual. The most touching expression that can be used to testify our sentiments towards Him may be but formulas uttered by the lips without moving our hearts; but sufferings endured for God, and sacrifices and crosses offered to Him, manifest more strikingly than words could, that we love Him purely for Himself. This is proof of our love—the one, too, which God desires, as it is given by the heart, whose most sensitive and delicate fibres, often bleeding and torn in nature's conflict, are looked upon with infinite appreciation by our divine Jesus, who will Himself in heaven become our only love and consolation.

THIRD POINT: The love of crosses and sufferings dilates our hearts, and rapidly increases the love of God in them. Those who fear crosses naturally shrink from the exercise of the works of mercy, from the frequent reception of the sacrament of penance, and the correction of their faults; whereas, love of sufferings removes all obstacles which retard, embarrass, and finally force us to desist entirely from the love of God. When the possession of earthly joys and benefits satisfies our hearts, we forget heaven; but when oppressed with sorrow and affliction, we instinctively draw nearer to God, and have recourse to prayer. When all around becomes dark, and, by providential concurrent circumstances or the heroism of our own will, we suffer in abandonment, then God becomes our resource, our support, and our hope; and the invocation, "Incline unto my aid, O God! O Lord! make haste to help me!" comes from the depths of our hearts. God manifests his love in a most tender and paternal manner towards those who generously suffer for him. This mercy of God removes the bitterness of sufferings without destroying it. The sting is felt, but the balm of divine consolation is immediately poured over to heal the wound. Thus suffering produces love, and love produces suffering in all souls, as well as in the soul of St. Joseph, whose heart was ever animated with divine love. Let us believe this doctrine and imitate this model.

PRAYER

HOLY St. Joseph, by our love for thee, and admiration of thy spirit of the cross, we beg of thee to obtain that our sentiments may become like unto thine. Thou couldst exclaim with the Prophet, *"Paratum cor meum, Deus, paratum cor meum*"—"My heart is ready, O Lord! my heart is ready." Then shall my soul be prepared for the loving designs of Providence, who realizes spiritual progress only by sacrifices and denials.

RESOLUTIONS

DURING the course of the day recall to mind the preceding reflections.

Repeat from time to time: *St. Joseph, ardent lover of God, pray for us.*

Let your mind and heart be impressed with the truths mentioned in the two preceding meditations.

Desire a more ardent love of God and of the cross.

Receive willingly and endure patiently all afflictions which God may send us.

Recite the *Our Father* and *Hail Mary* once, and *St. Joseph, pray for us*, three times.

Thirteenth Day

ST. JOSEPH, MODEL OF ARDENT CHARITY

❦

*Sancte Joseph, in charitate ardentissime,
ora pro nobis.*

St. Joseph, model of ardent charity, pray for us.

CHARITY is the most excellent and eminent of all virtues, including all the others, and giving them their true value and perfection. It is the noblest exercise of our faculties. Its influence produces the principal and essential difference between Christian virtue and human morality. Its practice is on earth, but its perfection only in heaven.

FIRST POINT: To love God seems simple and agreeable to the reasoning mind. God manifests himself in the beauty, grandeur, and sublimity of his wondrous works. Nevertheless, it is a remarkable fact that without the pale of the true religion, though we hear the word of God discussed in beautiful and appropriate terms, we seldom or never see manifest proofs of love towards Him. Natural strength and virtue are too weak to produce that act of supreme love which makes us prefer God above all things, and retain a deep and durable impression of love for Him; still it is not only possible, but easy, for a Christian to love God. Besides the eternal works of God, which always inspire one with an idea of His infinite perfections, a Christian has the revelations of faith opening to his view a new field vaster, a thousand times richer and more varied, whence shine forth the grandeur, beauty, and, above all, the goodness of God. Revelation is truly a field of mysteries, where all is splendor and beauty, greatness and sublimity; but let us repeat, more manifest than aught else, goodness and love. Moreover, as it is only by grace that the Christian is enabled to love God with his whole heart and soul, mind and strength—in a word, as God deserves to be loved—so those who do not correspond to this grace do not love God as he should be loved.

SECOND POINT: St. Joseph loved God with an ardent love. He was just; and perfect love of God and justice are inseparable. As he was eminently just, he loved the source of all justice in an eminent degree. Contemplating in their true light the grandeur and extent of the mysteries of Christianity, which are the sublimest testimony of the incomprehensible works of God and of his infinite bounty, he was attached to them by the closest and most tender ties. These sentiments were elevated and consecrated by an abundance of celestial favors and graces, greater than which were given to none but the Blessed Virgin Mary. How sweet to contemplate St. Joseph, not before the tabernacle where dwells the God of love, not at the foot of the cross whereon that God died for us, but carrying in his arms, and near his heart, the God Incarnate, the Infant God of love, who deigned and wished to be called the Son of Joseph. We are allowed to become participators in this happiness of our glorious saint by loving God with our whole souls.

THIRD POINT: Do we love God? Being Christians, we can and must love Him, and manifest our love by acts of love; saying our morning and evening prayers devoutly; loving Him above all things—that is to say, more than all the goods of the world, the interests of fortune, and more than anything created. We should love God with our whole hearts, not dividing our affections between the Creator and the creature, but loving all things in God and for Him, since our Lord Himself tells us we cannot serve two masters. We should love God with all our strength, not sparing ourselves in anything when the accomplishment of the will of God is concerned. We should love Him as the saints loved Him, as St. Joseph loved Him, and as did a holy priest, the Curé of Ars, who, with sweet simplicity, said, "God created little birds to sing, and they sing; God created man to love Him, and he does not love Him."

PRAYER

HOLY St. Joseph! my prayer today will be an act of love, which I will beg thee to present to God. I desire to love God, His holiness and infinite power. I desire to love the Sovereign Bounty, Him who is love, and who loves me with an ineffable love. In Him I will place my consolation and my strength here on earth, and my hope of supreme bliss in heaven.

RESOLUTIONS

DURING the course of the day recall to mind the preceding reflections.

Repeat from time to time the invocation: *St. Joseph, ardent lover of God, pray for us.*

Be diligent in the fulfillment of duty.

Sacrifice all affection for vain and trifling objects, and generously attach your hearts to the eternal welfare of your souls.

Do not listen to frivolous or uncharitable conversations.

Recite the *Our Father* and *Hail Mary* once, and *St. Joseph, pray for us*, three times.

Fourteenth Day

St. Joseph, Head of the Holy Family

⚜

Sancte Joseph, caput nobilissimæ et sanctissimæ familiæ, ora Pro nobis.

Saint Joseph, head of the holiest and noblest of families, pray for us.

IN our days, revolutions are everywhere rife. The spirit of revolt could not originate in society. It must be produced to a certain degree by the habits formed in family relations. In the family of Jesus, Mary, and Joseph we see order, peace, and calm serenity ruling all things. There neither talent nor merit claims the right of command; on the contrary, the greatest in merit and dignity obeys the least, and the will of God is the law of their lives. Let us examine each member of the Holy Family, and learn our duty from them.

First Point: *The Father.* He is the representative of God, the head and director of the household; but St. Joseph in this capacity exercises his authority with all simplicity, humility, and sweetness. He is continually brought before God by the weight of the double responsibility towards the Mother and the Child. Joseph was obedient to God in all things. He is the model after which fathers should govern. St. Paul warns them to avoid provoking impatience, anger or hatred by rough, harsh, irritable commands, or by the severity of their punishments, which are allowable only to repress disobedience or natural tendency to evil. Were the hearts of all fathers animated with the love of Jesus and of Mary, as was the heart of St. Joseph, their actions governed by the same principles, and their affections nourished by the same thoughts, their lives would close with the same desires.

Second Point: *The Mother.* All that Mary saw and heard was treasured in her heart, so that she might impart it to others. She allowed herself to be governed by St. Joseph without remark or resistance, well knowing the motives by which he was inspired. Whenever she interposed her authority, it was done by way of supplication, as at Cana, or by a tender maternal reproach, as in the temple. Silence, reserve, tears, and prayers should be the habitual resource of Christian mothers. A mother's sphere becomes extended when a father fails in his duty, compromises his authority, and even provokes resistance by his disorderly conduct. But we prefer to imagine ourselves in the heart of a Christian family, where the parents are all that God wishes them to be. A Catholic mother should imitate the Blessed Virgin in her prudence, reserve, and submission to the will of her husband; and the care of her children should be her chief duty. Though she exercises less authority over them than the father does, her influence is much greater than his. Oh! did mothers know the power of tears o'er the hearts of their children, and the efficacy of prayers in their behalf with the heart of Jesus, their lives would be offered a continual sacrifice for the salvation of those entrusted to their care.

THIRD POINT: *The Child.* Children should obey their parents. The only history of the childhood of Jesus given in the Gospel is, *Et erat subditus illus*—"And He was subject to them." It adds, it is true, that He grew in grace before God and man; but this was a consequence of His submission and obedience. The virtue of obedience comprises all the others. Children that are submissive and obedient to God and their parents will also increase in virtue, grace, and merit before God and man. Once only did our Lord seem to resist, or at least offer an excuse to His parents; when they complained of His having fled from them for three days, He said, "How is it that you sought me? Did you not know that I must be about my Father's business?" There is but one circumstance wherein a child is authorized to act contrary to the wishes of his parents: that is when the glory of God and the salvation of his soul is concerned. He should then say, as did Jesus, Do you not know that the interests of God, our Father in heaven, must first be considered, and that obedience to parents should be subordinate to the will of God?

PRAYER

GREAT Saint, not to thee alone do I this day address my prayer. I desire to invoke the whole family, of which you are the father. Holy and amiable family of Nazareth, Jesus, Mary, and Joseph, protect Christian families, particularly mine. Let humility, meekness, obedience, and all virtues dwell in it. May the members composing it be united in thee, that death may not separate them. May those bearing the cherished names of father, mother, brother, sister, or friend meet in heaven. Amen.

RESOLUTIONS

DURING the course of the day recall to your mind the preceding reflections.

Seek to learn from others, rather than to teach.

Be obedient to parents and superiors.

Mortify the sense of hearing.

Recite the *Our Father* and *Hail Mary* once, and *St. Joseph, pray for us*, three times.

St. Joseph, Model of the Hidden Life

❧

Sancte Joseph, caput nobilissimæ et sanctissimæ familiæ, ora Pro nobis.

Saint Joseph, head of the holiest and noblest of families, pray for us.

THE hidden life is fast becoming unknown, and every day we see less of it. Would that devotion to St. Joseph might bring persons to the practice of this life! The first cause detrimental to a hidden life is the aversion entertained by children for the occupation of parents, and the desire to withdraw themselves from their parental protection.

FIRST POINT: Let us contemplate the Holy Family of Nazareth; behold Jesus choosing His father's trade! He was an artisan and the son of an artisan. See St. Joseph, foster-father of the Infant God, become His instructor and His master; bringing Him up to labor, teaching Him His trade; and Jesus the while appearing to learn, as a testimony of affection and gratitude towards St. Joseph, rendering him and the Blessed Virgin all the assistance that a good son would give his parents. What a touching picture! Let us try to reproduce it in every family fireside, by advising children to consult God in prayer on the choice of a profession and state of life, and inculcating to them that wages may be used to advantage in every condition of life. Have those over whom you exercise influence cultivate habits of industry, and, if possible, have the daughter to pursue her occupations under the vigilance of her mother, the son to aid his father, and all to dwell together, rendering mutual services, which should be the honor and joy of a Christian family.

SECOND POINT: Family life is strengthened by a holy observance of the Sunday; that is to say, by refraining from servile works, assisting at Mass in the parish church, and seeking such amusements and relaxations as tend to unite the family circle. Let us contemplate the Holy Family at Nazareth, and draw from its example the confirmation of our opinion. In that admirable family no other absence is sought but that commanded by the law. Notice the sorrow and regret evinced by Mary and Joseph at Jerusalem for having lost the Child Jesus, though they could not have reproached themselves with negligence. See them together in the temple, at public prayer, at work, and at relaxations from duty. There was never a second occasion for the Blessed Virgin to search for her divine Son, whom she once supposed to be taken from her tender care. Christian parents and children, keep holy the Sabbath day! It is, by excellence, the day of the Lord; but it is also the day of rest for families. Remain in your own parish, let your recreations be holy, and taken as much as possible in common. O Christian parents! have you not often cause to search, weeping and sorrowful, for your children? The Blessed Virgin Mary and St.Joseph had no cause for anxiety concerning the soul of Jesus; but you, alas! on those festival days and evenings, when your children spend hours from home, have cause for anxious search in fear; for it is not the mortal life that is in danger, but the immortal souls of your precious charges.

THIRD POINT: Family ties are strengthened and affection nourished by the mutual interchange of thought, duties of respect towards the head of a family, instructions given to children, and the thousand other acts tending to attract the heart. Picture to yourselves the interior of the Holy Family at Nazareth! See Jesus, Mary, and Joseph at their meals, at work, and in conversation. What heavenly peace and consummate happiness, by the presence and union of the father, the mother, and the Child! Ah! could all families spend more time at the domestic fireside, and find there the rest and pleasure sought for elsewhere, how much happiness would be obtained for the thousand desolate homes whose members, carried away by love of dissipation and forbidden pleasures, bring sorrow and misery to their families!

PRAYER

HOLY St. Joseph! make us enter in spirit into the house of Nazareth, honored by so many mysteries, but especially by the hidden life you led there for many years with Jesus and Mary. Obtain for us from the hearts of Jesus and Mary an esteem for a hidden life, and the desire of practising it after their example, with the interior virtues necessary for so holy an enterprise.

RESOLUTIONS

PREPARE to receive Holy Communion on the feast of St. Joseph.

Conform your will to the will of others.

Sacrifice personal tastes to the pleasure of others.

Seek the good of others at the cost of your own inclinations.

Recite the *Our Father* and *Hail Mary* once, and *St. Joseph, pray for us*, three times.

Sixteenth Day

St. Joseph, Model of Justice

❈

Sancte Joseph, fabrorum et operariorum exemplar,
ora pro nobis.

St. Joseph, model of artisans and workmen,
pray for us.

FIRST POINT: Jesus and Joseph were artisans. Divine Providence selected this condition of life for them, in order to honor and sanctify manual labor for them, which the nations of antiquity regarded as mean and debasing. Jesus and Joseph are in this capacity presented as models to those who earn their bread in the sweat of their brow. Laborers and mechanics participate more fully in the blessings promised in the Gospel to the poor than do those in more elevated positions, for they have less to fear from the curse that falls on the abuse of riches. True, their condition is in itself painful and unpleasant to nature, particularly at times when work fails or salaries decrease so as not to meet demands of maintenance; yet in those trials they ought to be encouraged and consoled by the example of these great models, Jesus and Joseph. Let them choose St. Joseph for their patron and protector. Jesus, our divine Saviour, gave up the employment of a mechanic during the last three years of his life, in order to attend to his divine mission; but St. Joseph continued his labors until his death, and he was known among his contemporaries as Joseph the carpenter.

SECOND POINT: The duties of a laborer or mechanic are: order and regularity in his habits of life, strict honesty in his commercial relations, a detestation of the use of false weights and measures, and of deception in any form. He was an honest and noble mechanic, or, in the widest acceptation of the expression, was just by excellence. Admire the sublime elevation of soul manifested in this holy descendant of Juda's kings. When we see him labor with his hands for maintenance, we perceive the nobility of character, purity of conscience, and delicacy of sentiment exhibited in the self-sacrificing spirit of the spouse of the most pure Virgin. What admirable simplicity portrayed in his obedience to the mandate of the sovereign and the laws of the country, even at the risk of excessive fatigue to the Blessed Virgin, who bore the Son of God in her most chaste womb!

THIRD POINT: The secret of this ennobling and sanctifying influence on the actions of St. Joseph, even in his obscure condition, is the purity of intention which directed his every work. It is well known that the virtues of the Blessed Virgin and of St. Joseph were not made less brilliant by the obscurity of their lives; for in the sight of God, the Supreme and Eternal Truth, Mary and Joseph were higher than the greatest sovereigns. Self-love suffices to obscure the most meritorious and brightest act; and though the hidden virtues are less liable to be wrought upon by the fatal illusions of self-love, still they are not entirely safe from its baneful influence, unless we keep constant watch over the movements of our hearts. We must strive to acquire the habit of virtue, so that the good may predominate in us. Our actions become the more meritorious, and the virtuous habits acquired are the more elevated, according as our intention is centred in God. Of all the supernatural motives, that of charity is most capable of inciting our souls to good. We should offer to God every act, however insignificant, and let love for him animate every thought, word, and action. The poor and lowly can become great in merit and virtue, as did St. Joseph. They can imitate him as their model, and invoke him as their protector.

PRAYER

HOLY St. Joseph, be the protector and model of all those who are obliged to labor for the support of their families. Teach them to fulfil their duties in a Christian manner; recall to their minds in what true greatness consists; and obtain for them fidelity to your example. May they learn from you that the secret of true happiness, even here on earth, is moderation of desires, patience, resignation, the hope of heaven, and the joy of loving and serving God.

RESOLUTIONS

AVOID all conversations having a tendency to make you dissatisfied with your condition in life.

Let the poor and lowly thank God for having called them to a state of poverty, and those favored with wealth and luxury beg of God to enable them to use these gifts for their eternal salvation.

Do not seek for dainties to satisfy your palate.

Recite the *Our Father* and *Hail Mary* once, and *St. Joseph, pray for us*, three times.

St. Joseph, Model of Charity Towards our Neighbor

✠

Sancte Joseph, in charitate ardentissime,
ora pro nobis.

St. Joseph, model of charity towards our
neighbor, pray for us.

WE will now consider St. Joseph in his relations with his neighbor. As a carpenter, a voluntary exile, and a citizen of his native country, he proves to us, by his example, that of all the duties we owe to our neighbor, charity is the first.

FIRST POINT: The law of charity binds us equally towards God and our neighbor. It might be deemed necessary to use a different term by which to designate the supreme and absolute love we have for God in distinction from that we bear towards our neighbor. But to separate the love of God from the love of our neighbor would be to deny the nature of love, which engages the dearest and most intense affections of the heart, and which disposes us to forget and sacrifice ourselves for those we love. The second commandment is like unto the first, says our Saviour, so much so that its origin and its end are the same, for it is the image, the will, the love of God; in a word, it is God whom we love in our neighbor. We cannot separate the love of God and the love of our neighbor, for loving our neighbor in a Christian manner is loving God. "Thou shalt love the Lord thy God with thy whole heart, thy whole mind, thy whole strength, and thy neighbor as thyself." This precept is the expressed command of our Saviour, strictly recommended to us, and its fulfilment will be the badge by which the disciples of Jesus Christ will be known. The heart of St. Joseph was inspired with this tender and devoted love for the whole human family.

SECOND POINT: We must practice charity in our relations with our friends and enemies. It seems unnecessary for us to mention the duty of love for friends. Our Lord says, "If you love them that love you, what reward shall you have? Do not even the publicans this?" It is precisely that your friendship may not be similar to that of the pagans that your thoughts, affections, and hearts are referred to the example of St. Joseph. In his humble condition his friends were few. None are mentioned in the Gospel, unless it be that the title may be given to the shepherds and wise men who came to Bethlehem. Friendships which are produced by love of pleasure, sympathy of character, business relations, or natural affection independent of a higher and holier aim, have not love of God for their motive. The Gospel, moreover, commands us not only to forgive our enemies, and pray for them, but also to love them. This precept is violated by a great number of Christians. We entertain and manifest cold reserve and resentment towards those who have offended or injured us; yet each day we say, "Forgive us our trespasses as we forgive them that trespass against us." These words should be dwelt upon until we are well impressed with their import.

THIRD POINT: We owe the duty of charity towards all mankind. St. Joseph greeted his neighbor with a friendly smile, evoked by love; and as no one was excluded from the love of Jesus, neither did St. Joseph deny his love to any one. Wherever Providence placed him, all manifested indifference towards him on account of his poverty, but he in return regarded them with affection, and desired their salvation. Let us strive to benefit some one each day of our lives, either by prayers or example, being particularly kind to those who offend us or manifest ingratitude towards us, and let us be convinced that Jesus Christ and His love are sufficient for us.

PRAYER

GLORIOUS St. Joseph, thy name is synonymous with sweetness and charity. Each word of the Gospel concerning thee seems to exhale the perfume of these amiable virtues. Pray for us that we may imitate thee in the avoidance of discontent, impatience, jealousy, hatred, bitterness, violence, and resentment, and obtain that our whole lives be animated by charity, that at death we may be received with mercy and love by the God of love.

RESOLUTIONS

DURING the course of the day recall to mind the preceding reflections.

Repeat from time to time the invocation: *St. Joseph, meek and humble, pray for us.*

Rejoice in the good of others.

Pardon all injuries.

Recite the *Our Father* and *Hail Mary* once, and *St. Joseph, pray for us*, three times.

Eighteenth Day

St. Joseph, Model of Humility

❧

*Sancte Joseph, in humilitate profundissime,
ora pro nobis.*

St. Joseph, profoundly humble, pray for us.

FIRST POINT: The principal virtue in our relations with our neighbor is humility. This virtue, so little known among the generality of worldlings, is of purely Christian origin. We will speak here of a few of its characteristic traits.

Humility is the acquiescence of the mind and heart to the knowledge of our own misery and nothingness. Whatever increases and strengthens this knowledge may serve in some measure to develop one or more of the qualities of humility. In the first place, frequent reflection on the infinite greatness of God contributes much to this virtue, placing before our minds the contrast which naturally arises from the thought of His infinite perfections and our own unworthiness. We are but creatures, holding all we have from God. "What have you that you have not received?" says St. Paul. This reflection serves to maintain in us sentiments of the most profound humility. We have, perhaps, offended God grievously; and in consequence of the inclination to evil which we find in ourselves, in spite of all our resolutions, we still continue to fall into many faults. "The just man falls seven times," says the wise man. We can of ourselves do nothing towards our eternal salvation, not even form a good thought, without the aid of that all-powerful Being who created us. God must aid and support us in the accomplishment of all the good we do, and yet how have we corresponded to this grace? Here are motives on which we can and must rely, particularly on the last, in order to be convinced of our spiritual misery. However, to have humility, it is not sufficient to acquiesce with the mind alone to the knowledge just mentioned; for that of the heart is also necessary, inasmuch as we must not revolt or complain, but submit and be resigned, and even go so far as to desire to be perfectly well known and treated as we deserve. This is the sense conveyed in the expression of our Saviour, "Learn of me, for I am meek and humble of heart." This divine lesson, so difficult on account of the innate pride in us, we also receive, and should learn, from St. Joseph, who obtained it from the loving heart of Jesus, and we should earnestly implore Him to impart the secret of acquiring it to us.

SECOND POINT: We have said that after charity, humility, more than all the other virtues, enables us to regulate our conduct towards our neighbor. The words of our divine Saviour already quoted will make this more clearly understood: "Learn of me, for I am meek and humble of heart, and you will find rest for your souls." The word meek, used by Jesus before that of humble, and the words terminating the quotation, reveal to us, in all its beauty, the doctrine we are to explain. Meekness, that virtue which of itself affords inexpressible delight, accompanied, as it is, by the promise of so great a reward, seems to be, by excellence, the virtue most needed for the gaining of our neighbor. Has not our Lord Himself said, "Blessed are the meek, for they shall possess the land;" or, in other words, Blessed are the meek, for they shall possess the heart of man? Meekness, says St. Francis de Sales, is the sister or flower of charity; but, mark well, we cannot be meek or even good Christians unless we are humble, and we will certainly be meek if we are humble of heart. Humility, then, such as we have characterized in the first point, must necessarily be accompanied by meekness. Have we understood it thus, and endeavored to make this our constant practice and the rule of our conduct towards our neighbor? Does our humility tend to bring him joy, calm, and peace? Does it afford rest to our own souls ?

THIRD POINT: This examination of ourselves is painful, because humiliating; and perhaps we are not yet sufficiently humble to undergo it as we should. Let us rest our minds and hearts in beholding a touching model of humility! Let us contemplate St. Joseph in the different conditions in which he was placed by divine Providence, and see his lowly humility! Not a word of complaint ever escaped him; no regret for the departed grandeur of his family; no thought of complacency on the mission fulfilled by him; he considers himself only as the servant and dispenser of the things confided to him. He conforms in all things to the divine will, never murmuring under the many crosses placed upon him. Meek and forbearing towards all, in humility he possessed his soul. Here is your model. In what do you resemble him? Implore his assistance in overcoming your many defects.

PRAYER

O DEAR St. Joseph! grant that by thy example and that of my divine Saviour I may become meek and humble of heart. Thou, who in this wert a faithful imitator of Jesus, cause these virtues to enter deeply into my soul, and grant that by the practice of them I may become more and more like thee. I abandon myself to thee, and invoke thy aid. This lesson of humility is one of the most difficult in the Gospel; but nothing is impossible to God. And thou wilt be for me an all-powerful suppliant at the throne of grace, whence my soul may be imbued with meekness and humility. Amen.

RESOLUTIONS

DURING the course of the day recall to mind the preceding reflections.

Repeat from time to time: *St. Joseph, meek and humble, pray for us.*

Convince yourself of your miseries by reflecting on the goodness of God and your ingratitude.

Willingly accept the humiliations that may befall you.

Recite the *Our Father* and *Hail Mary* once, and *St. Joseph, pray for us*, three times.

Nineteenth Day

St. Joseph, Model of Religious

❦

Sancte Joseph, vir juste atque perfecte, ora pro nobis.

Saint Joseph, just and perfect man, pray for us.

FIRST POINT: A religious vows the practice of the evangelical counsels by subjecting himself in a particular manner to perfect obedience. The Gospel does not tell us that St. Joseph contracted any such engagements, but we infer from tradition that he made a vow of chastity. Whatever may have been the nature of the promises by which he bound himself to God, the perfection of his life gives him a close resemblance to religious, and he is proposed to them as a model. A religious makes the three vows of poverty, chastity, and obedience. St. Joseph was poor, chaste, and obedient; but, at the same time, his manner and condition of life give him as a model to persons living in the world, and who wish to serve God more perfectly than the generality of Christians, and to add the practice of counsels to the virtue of precept.

You who have made sacred engagements with God, renew them now with special fervor, and place them under the protection of St. Joseph. You who feel in your hearts the desire of leading a more perfect life by applying yourselves to the realization of the virtues, spirit, and the perfection of religious, invoke your father, St. Joseph, for you are of his family. And you who live the ordinary lives of Christians, and do not feel yourselves called to the practice of the counsels, be faithful in fulfilling all the commandments required of you; for in this way progress will be gained each day, and at last a relative perfection will be attained. Not to advance is to recede. Place yourselves today under his protection, and on this his feast day his holy prayers will serve as a support to yours.

SECOND POINT: No religious, by the fulfillment of his vows, has ever attained so high a degree of perfection as St. Joseph. Living in the world, surrounded by the objects from which a religious separates himself, and even possessing them; reserving rights which the religious renounces, St. Joseph, by a continual self-denial and entire abandonment to the will of God, practised the three virtues of poverty, chastity, and obedience in all that was in them most difficult, pure, and elevated. He was, it is true, proprietor of his little home and his working-tools, but his was an ownership detached from all things, willing to be in exile, and ready to remove wherever and whenever God desired him. St. Joseph was a husband, and he lived with his chaste spouse as her guardian, consoler, protector, and support. But he was the virginal spouse of the most pure Virgin. He commanded because he was the head of a family, the care of which was given him; and though he held the authority until his latest breath, he nevertheless was most obedient, since he conformed himself to all the orders of Providence, and accomplished them with precision and eagerness, as is testified by the words of the Gospel. Let us imitate this beautiful model.

THIRD POINT: In order to understand the degree of religious perfection attained by St. Joseph, we must consider that he was not sustained by any of those human motives which faith may countenance, though they be detrimental to perfection, since they afford natural pleasure. His life was hidden and unknown. He cared not for fame, nor for friendly encouragement, nor human patronage. The joy of a good conscience, the satisfaction of having fulfilled his duty, and the love of God, were sufficient for him. In this he is a model for religious and all persons engaged by vow to the service of God. Let us examine the motive by which we are animated. If it be solely with a view of pleasing God and testifying our love for Him, let us thank God for giving us grace to act thus. Let us not allow human motives to influence nor detract from vows so noble, pure, and sacred that we offer to God in testimony of our love for Him; and those in the world who live without having made any formal engagement binding them to the practice of the counsels and perfection should know that St. Joseph occupied a position similar to theirs, and that, though he made no religious vow, he was nevertheless more perfect than they are. Imitate him by daily aspiring to a closer union with Jesus Christ and fidelity to the inspirations of conscience.

PRAYER

O BLESSED Joseph! since Jesus while on earth was subject to thee, rendered prompt obedience to thy commands, and cherished thee with most especial love and honor, how shall He now refuse thee anything in heaven, where all thy merits receive their full reward? Pray for me, therefore, holy patriarch, and obtain for me these necessary graces: first of all, that I may have a sincere contrition for my sins; that I may ever hate and fear all that is evil, and flee from it with firmness and constancy, especially from my most besetting sins; grant that I may amend my life daily more and more, and constantly apply myself to the acquiring of virtue, especially those virtues I need most; and that I may be kept safe amid the various temptations and occasions by which my soul may be exposed to the peril of damnation. For these and for all other needful graces, O holy Joseph! I commend myself to the goodness and mercy of my God, and to thy fatherly care and intercession! Amen.

RESOLUTIONS

DURING the course of the day recall to mind the preceding reflections.

Repeat from time to time the invocation: *St. Joseph, model of all virtues, pray for us.*

Do not regard stubbornness and obstinacy as dignity of character; but let sincerity and goodness, or rather humility and meekness, be the true dignity we will strive to attain.

Make some sacrifice that will enable you to lay aside an alms for the Holy Father.

Recite the *Our Father* and *Hail Mary* once, and *St. Joseph, pray for us*, three times.

Twentieth Day

St. Joseph, Model
of Obedience

✣

Sancte Joseph, vir obedientissime, ora pro nobis.

St. Joseph, most obedient, pray for us.

FIRST POINT: *The necessity of obedience.* Every man is obliged to obey. Every Christian should render implicit obedience to the commands of God and of His Church. We have previously considered the duty of children to obey their parents; we will now consider the obligation of obedience which binds us all. To obey is incumbent on all men. Though God does not Himself confer with us, nor send special messengers to us, as he did to Joseph, nevertheless He gives us His law, and manifests himself to us through His Church in the teaching of His ministers; therefore the fulfilling of our duties is but an act of obedience.

Moreover, all are, in a measure, dependent on certain authorities, and, be these civil, religious, or parental, we are bound in justice to render obedience to them. We obey God when we submit to lawful authority; and, on the contrary, when we refuse to obey those whom the will of God has placed over us, we disobey God Himself. St. Joseph obeyed the mandate of the Emperor Augustus in going to Bethlehem; but he had in view an authority far superior to that of a worldly prince, for he recognized the will of God in the command of his earthly ruler.

SECOND POINT: *Advantages of obedience.* Scripture says, "An obedient man shall speak of victory." In fact, the victory gained over self-love and pride in rendering obedience to others, and submitting our will to theirs, immeasurably multiplies the triumphs of a Christian, and these triumphs may be gained each day. According to another passage found in Scripture, "Obedience is better than sacrifice." In explanation of this text, St. Gregory says in the immolation of victims, it is the flesh of animals that is offered to God;

whereas, by obedience we sacrifice ourselves. The merit of one act of obedience may be extended to a series of acts, and serve to consecrate them all to God; sometimes one act devotes an entire life to God. Thus St. Joseph, by obeying the orders of the emperor, procured the fulfillment of all the prophecies concerning the birth of our Saviour. By his flight into Egypt, he consecrated several years of his life to the accomplishment of the designs of God. We should be grateful to God for giving us a means whereby to acknowledge our desire of submitting to His will, in the prayer He taught His disciples: "Thy will be done on earth as it is in heaven." We should say these words with a lively feeling of our dependence on Him.

THIRD POINT: *Qualities of Obedience.* St. Joseph obeyed in spirit and in truth. He followed the dictates of his conscience in the sight of God, and with the desire of pleasing Him; not caring how men should regard him, nor had he any fear of creating their displeasure, nor the desire of attracting their attention and admiration. St. Joseph obeyed promptly. The

Scripture assures us that he executed the orders of God at the instant that they were manifested to him. What homage and love we may render to God by this ready obedience, and what a source of graces is opened for us if we submit promptly to the will of those authorized by our heavenly Father to command us! Love was the motive and principle of the obedience of Joseph. Where love is, obedience is sweet. All who are lawfully placed in authority hold their position by the will of God; and even though they be harsh, severe, morose, and unkind, still they should be obeyed, on the consideration that God wills us to be subject to them, and thereby prove our love for Him.

PRAYER

HOLY St. Joseph, obtain for me the true spirit of obedience. Help me to subdue my pride and submit my will freely to the salutary yoke of obedience. Let my soul be animated by a humility like unto that of our Mother Mary when she said: "Behold the handmaid of the Lord; be it done unto me according to Thy word"; and pray that I may understand the advantages and necessity of faithful obedience. Amen.

RESOLUTIONS

DURING the course of the day recall to mind the preceding reflections.

Repeat from time to time: *St. Joseph, model of obedience, pray for us.*

Conform your will to the will of your superiors.

Render a prompt and loving obedience to those who command you.

Recite the *Our Father* and *Hail Mary* once, and *St. Joseph, pray for us,* three times.

St. Joseph, Model of Religious Obedience

❧

Sancte Joseph, vir obedientissime, ora pro nobis.

St. Joseph, most obedient, pray for us.

OBEDIENCE is a virtue which imparts peace to the faithful soul, be he religious or secular. Ecclesiastics and religious are indeed happy in the certainty of always performing the will of God by obeying their rules and superiors.

FIRST POINT: *Obedience practised by Superiors.* Superiors have some higher authority to whom they owe subjection. Even the princes of the earth have superiors in those who direct them in either spiritual or temporal matters. It is a relief for those who command to feel that they are dependent on some one, whom they are to obey. To go still further, they can practice this virtue not only by obeying their superiors and equals, but in a manner their inferiors, by listening with kind attention to them, and never making them feel their inferiority. Jesus Christ himself teaches this in his conduct towards St. Joseph, and the life of this holy patriarch presents many examples of this admirable virtue.

SECOND POINT: *Superiors and parents, when commanding, should seek only the greater glory of God.* With this disposition of mind and this intention in view, they will find that in commanding others they are invariably obeying God. The faithful practice of these two principles will give the command a mildness and force which it would not otherwise possess. Let us contemplate St. Joseph as superior in his domestic capacity over Jesus and Mary, and admire his sweetness and humility. He is our model. Do we resemble him?

THIRD POINT: *Parents and superiors—in fact, all who are placed over others—should have specified rules for the regulation of their different actions and exercises of each day.* Thus, in the morning, they should strive to foresee all that may happen before evening, and thereby prevent many faults of inadvertence. Besides, by having a specified time for each action, they will have frequent occasion of exercising their fidelity in the practice of obedience. Again, contemplate St. Joseph in the cottage at Nazareth, dwelling with Jesus and Mary. Order and regularity attend his every action. He has a specified time for rising, for prayer, for meals, work, relaxation, and even for repose. The Gospel, telling of their journey to Jerusalem, says: "And when he was twelve years old, they were going up into Jerusalem, according to the custom of the feast, and having fulfilled the days"; and from this we may infer that all their actions were regulated according to rule.

PRAYER

ST. JOSEPH, admirable model of obedience, teach me to obey like thee; grant that, in commanding others, I myself may not lose the spirit of obedience. Assist me, I beseech thee, dear Saint, and with thy aid I will be sure of success.

RESOLUTIONS

DURING the course of the day recall to mind the preceding reflections.

Accustom your mind to view the will of God in the orders of your superiors.

Be particularly faithful to your rule.

Recite the Psalm "*Miserere*" on your knees.

Recite the *Our Father* and *Hail Mary* once, and *St. Joseph, pray for us,* three times.

Twenty-second Day

ST. JOSEPH, DEPOSITARY OF THE SECRETS OF GOD

※

Sancte Joseph, coadjutor magni consilii, ora pro nobis.

St. Joseph, depositary of great designs,
pray for us.

FIRST POINT: The first great design in which St. Joseph co-operated was the sanctification of his soul. God created us without our co-operation, but He will not justify us without it. The greater the graces and privileges received, the more humble and earnest must be our endeavors to correspond with them. The creature has nothing for commendation in himself for the concurring in these graces; on the contrary, he should fear lest sufficient has not been done on his part. St. Joseph understood perfectly well the necessity of this co-operation. Penetrated with gratitude for the favors he had received, he strove only to correspond faithfully with them. We must likewise concur in the great design of our sanctification. God has made known to us, by innumerable lights and graces, that He wishes us to become partakers of His happiness and glory. He purifies us from our faults, offers us every means of obtaining pardon, assists us in acquiring virtue, and, above all, the virtue of charity. It was charity that caused Him to reveal Himself to us, to assume our weak nature, becoming man for our salvation. *Deus charitas est*— "God is charity." Do we comprehend the sublimity of our destiny, and strive to attain it? The grace of God is necessary to advance in perfection, but our co-operation is required. The grace of God is with me, says St. Paul.

SECOND POINT: St. Joseph was made participator in another great design of God: the care of Jesus, the Incarnate Word, and Mary, the most perfect of all creatures, masterpiece of the hand of God, purer and more exalted than the angels. The intimate, minute, and deep knowledge which he obtained of them was revealed to him by degrees. The angels, shepherds, and wise men, the voice of the multitude, the interior lights, but, above all, his thirty years' residence with them, which the angels themselves might have envied, served to show to St. Joseph the mysteries of grace and love attached to the persons of Jesus and Mary. This successive and gradual knowledge gave place to transports of admiration and delight. What must have been the happiness of St. Joseph in being so closely united to Him whom the angels and saints revere, and before whom they bow in lowly adoration! We may not be able to obtain the same degree of knowledge of these two beings, yet we can and should study daily to make progress in it. For have we not the Gospel explained and interpreted by the Church; the lives of the saints, which are reflections of the lives of Jesus and his holy Mother? We have, above all, the Holy Eucharist; and where can be found more touching or more admirable remembrances of Nazareth ?

THIRD POINT: The third mystery in which St. Joseph was made a participator was that of which St. Paul speaks when he says, "And evidently great is the mystery of godliness which was manifested in the flesh, justified in the spirit, appeared unto angels, hath been preached unto the Gentiles, is believed in the world, is taken up in glory." The Incarnation, united with Redemption, for the salvation of the whole world, is the mystery in which St. Joseph, after the Blessed Virgin, became participator. He aided, by his obedience, zeal, and prudence, in the accomplishment of these designs; he contracted engagements with God which served to attach him to all mankind, rendering him in some manner responsible for each one of us, and even for the existence of our adorable Saviour. We, in turn, are obliged to cooperate by word and example in the fruits and effects of these mysteries. The mystery of the Incarnation is forcibly brought to the mind each day as we repeat the *Angelus*, "And the Word was made flesh, and dwelt among us." This part of the *Angelus*, fervently said, may be offered up by the pious soul in reparation for the affronts offered to the Redeemer by the taunts of the impious, the contempt of the infidel, the forgetfulness of the tepid, and the indifference of so many relaxed Christians.

PRAYER

HOLY St. Joseph! my mind is deeply penetrated with the thoughts of these great truths; but I need the inspirations of divine grace to be faithful to the inspirations received. Do thou obtain for me that, like thee, I may faithfully concur in the designs of God. Amen.

RESOLUTIONS

DURING the course of the day recall to mind the preceding reflections.

From time to time repeat: *St. Joseph, faithful to divine grace, pray for us.*

Carefully banish all distractions during prayer.

Avoid deliberate sins.

Recite the *Our Father* and *Hail Mary* once, and *St. Joseph, pray for us*, three times.

Twenty-third Day

ST. JOSEPH, MODEL OF PRUDENCE

❦

Sancte Joseph, vir prudentissime, ora pro nobis.

St. Joseph, model of prudence, pray for us.

FIRST POINT: Prudence is a virtue which causes us to use the most appropriate means whereby to arrive at a proposed end. Prudence is a virtue old as the world. The Bible affords us admirable models of prudence. The first Joseph offers an example of this virtue unequalled in history, unless it be by the second Joseph, who signalized himself no less than the first by the prudent management of all confided to him. We have seen St. Joseph correspond with the designs of God in an admirable and perfect manner, and this correspondence was the fruit of his prudence. This is a necessary virtue, since one

who is just and faithful to God is directed by it
in the solution of the most delicate, important,
and elevated questions. Our Saviour Himself
tells us, "Be prudent as the serpent and simple
as the dove." As the eyes of the servant never
close completely, so prudence must always
watch and rule our desires, words, and actions.

SECOND POINT: There are two kinds of
prudence—worldly prudence and a prudence
coming from God; and it is necessary to
discriminate between them. Worldly
prudence, not having an object in view similar
to Christian prudence, looks to the attainment
of worldly advantages, and places the joy and
happiness of man in the possession of them, not
caring by what means this end be obtained, and
fearing only the censure of public opinion and
the law. The success attendant on this worldly
prudence seems to justify its practice; and its
possessors fear nothing more than want of
capacity, which they term a fault compromising
them in the eyes of men; hence they avoid it.
Have we to accuse ourselves of practising this

prudence by allowing worldly motives to direct our actions? The first Joseph was chosen by Pharaoh to teach prudence to the wise men of the court. Let us learn this virtue from our father, St. Joseph.

THIRD POINT: Christian prudence, unlike the one above mentioned, proposes for its aim the eternal salvation of the soul, the glory of God, and the accomplishment of His adorable will. Even when regarding temporal, material, social, or political matters, Christian prudence always looks beyond the terrestrial aim. This is the first law of Christian prudence. As to the means made use of for the attaining of the proposed end, it draws them from the rules laid down in the Gospel, and from the examples contained therein. In selecting from them, it accepts only those which conscience regards as perfectly legitimate. Blending humility with these, it fears not any threatened misfortunes, seeks not to avoid them by making use of expedients injurious not only to sanctity, but also to the dignity of a Christian. In working for God, a zeal enlightened by divine inspiration and directed by obedience is sure of success. St. Joseph is an admirable model of Christian prudence, the only one deserving of the name of a prudent man in its complete acceptation. St. Joseph was a simple, upright, and God-fearing man. His simplicity was not the result of a weak mind or judgment, but proceeded from the Dispenser of all graces, and was bestowed for our example. How may we imitate this sublime model?

PRAYER

PRUDENT saint! obtain for me the spirit of true simplicity. I have compromised by repeated infidelities, and have not made the proper use of, the means placed at my disposal for the attaining of this end by an all-wise Providence. Aid me, kind protector, to amend my life. Impress deeply on my heart the nothingness of earth and the importance of my eternal salvation.

RESOLUTIONS

DURING the course of the day recall to mind the preceding reflections.

Follow the advice of a director.

Recite the *Our Father* and *Hail Mary* once, and *St. Joseph, pray for us*, three times.

Twenty-fourth Day

St. Joseph, Model of Chastity

❈

Sancte Joseph, vir virgo virginis matris, ora pro nobis.

St. Joseph, virgin spouse of a Virgin Mother,
pray for us.

FIRST POINT: *The vow of virginity uniting Joseph and Mary.* We have already spoken of the title, Spouse of Mary, conferred on St. Joseph—a title which was the first and essential basis of his greatness. A virgin should have a virginal spouse; and there is every reason to believe, independently of Scripture, that St. Joseph had taken the vow of chastity. The bond was reciprocal, and the marriage of Joseph and Mary served only to unite them more closely, and establish a mutual desire for the spiritual good of each other. "They are virgins uniting themselves," says Bossuet, "and, like two bright stars, imparting their light to each other." St. Joseph united to the Blessed Virgin is a model which all married persons should strive to imitate. Regulating their lives, words, and actions in accordance with this model, they need not fear being led astray from the path of holiness.

SECOND POINT: *Honor of the title of virgin.* Barrenness in a family was regarded by the Jews as a dishonor, or at least a severe trial. We read in the old law of several just persons who accepted this trial with submission, but not without bitter regret. We have a touching example of this in the person of Anna, the mother of Samuel. Among the just who lived before the coming of our Saviour, Scripture does not mention any one who bound himself by vow to the practice of chastity. St. Joseph and the Blessed Virgin were the first. Let us congratulate and honor them as the recipients of this most glorious of all privileges. Virginity is the highest state of life to which a creature can be called. If we have the happiness of being called to this state, let us thank our divine Saviour for bestowing on us this greatest of graces. The married state is also holy, and is ranked by Jesus Christ among the sacraments, and sanctified in the Church by prayer. Virginity is holier, as is proved by the words of St. Paul: "Therefore, both he that giveth his virgin in marriage doth well, and he that giveth her not doth better." Each individual is in duty bound to correspond as well as he is able to his vocation.

THIRD POINT: *Reward of the virginity of St. Joseph.* The special privilege of being called the foster-father of Jesus Christ and the guardian of the Holy Virgin was a reward of his virginity, as was also the inexpressible honor given him of having Jesus repose on his virginal heart. By this first example of virginity given to the world, St. Joseph became the father and guardian of all who make a similar vow. Virgins, as spouses of Jesus, should carefully guard and cherish this virtue, inasmuch as they are obliged to instill a love and respect for it into the hearts of those under their care, and knowing that the more they themselves love, revere, and practise it, the greater will be their influence over others, and the greater their reward in eternity.

PRAYER

O THOU who gavest St. Joseph to Mary for a protector, and who didst favor the heart of this great saint by making it the first adorer of the Heart of Jesus in the bosom of his mother, grant that by his prayers and by imitating him I may dwell with him in the heart of the Immaculate Virgin, there to adore God for ever. Amen.

RESOLUTIONS

D URING the course of the day recall to mind the preceding reflections.

Repeat often the invocation: *St. Joseph, model of chaste souls, pray for us.*

Pray for humility.

Repeat occasionally the words of St. Paul: "Lord! what wilt thou have me do?"

Observe modesty of the eyes.

Recite the *Our Father* and *Hail Mary* once, and *St. Joseph, pray for us*, three times.

Twenty-fifth Day

St. Joseph, Model of Purity

✥

Sancte Joseph, vir virgo virginis matris, ora pro nobis.

St. Joseph, virgin spouse of a Virgin Mother,
pray for us.

FIRST POINT: *Beauty of the virtue of purity.* This heavenly virtue renders us dear to God and to men. Blessed are the clean of heart, for they shall see God. The perfume of this virtue is the most agreeable that can be offered to God. Purity assimilates man unto the angels. In praising purity, it is St. Joseph we eulogize. Virgin spouse of a Virgin Mother, pray for us. Preserve childhood inviolate in mind and heart, protect youth, support mature age; and may the aged, through thy protection, add to their crowns gems of unsullied radiant purity.

SECOND POINT: *The contrary vice.* Where is the painter who can find figures sufficiently dark and horrible wherewith to picture the contrary vice? God cursed it in the beginning of time in these terrible words: "My spirit shall not remain in man for ever, because he is flesh!" God has punished it with fearful chastisements. In order to efface its stain from the earth, the Deluge was sent; the cities of Sodom and Gomorrah were destroyed by fire; a whole tribe among the Israelites was annihilated on account of the sin of a few; David, the prophet king, chosen by God himself, was rigorously chastised for his sin by the loss of his kingdom and the death of his son. Solomon, the wisest of kings, died leaving the world uncertain as to his destiny. The list of chastisements by which God punished, even here on earth, the vice of impurity is inexhaustible. If God sometimes delays the punishment, it is not the less certain nor terrible. Woe to him who, for the gratification of sensuality, brings sin and disgrace to an accomplice, or, worse still, to a poor victim. The punishment given on earth to such is remorse of conscience; and when this remorse is crushed, the neglect of religious practices follows, which is succeeded by loss of faith and, finally, that spiritual blindness which gives the sign of reprobation. Chaste spouse of a Virgin Mother, pray for and protect us.

THIRD POINT: *Means of preserving purity.* Watching, mortification, and prayer. Our enemy goes about like a roaring lion, seeking whom he may devour; and he must be resisted with the arms of faith, which are fasting, watching, and prayer. Our Lord himself tells us, when speaking of the demon of impurity, "This kind of demon can be expelled only by prayer and fasting." According to the interpretation of the Church of these words, fasting embraces all kinds of mortification and sacrifices. We have endeavored, during this month, to initiate you into the practice of mortification and sacrifices that could not injure your health nor interfere with the duties of your state of life. Let us strive to impress our minds with these thoughts and the salutary effects of these practices, so that we may derive lasting benefit from them, and make use of them in time of temptation, and at the same time be impressed with the truth that humility is necessary for us. The humble alone pass unsullied through this sort of temptation. Add to sacrifice, humility, and mortification morning and evening prayers, the sign of the cross in time of temptation, the invocation of the sweet names, Jesus, Mary, and Joseph, and the words of the Lord's Prayer, "Lead us not into temptation." But all these will not suffice if we do not guard our imagination and senses. "Watch and pray, that ye enter not into temptation." Parents, watch over your children; be their visible guardian angels, their second providences. Masters and mistresses, watch over and correct the disorders of your household; for nothing can escape the all-seeing eye of God, and you must account to Him at the tribunal of justice.

PRAYER

REMEMBER, O amiable and powerful protector, St. Joseph! that according to the testimony of your devoted servant, St. Teresa, no one ever implored your intercession with devotion and confidence without obtaining relief. Animated by this sweet and consoling hope, I come to you, O worthy spouse of the Virgin of virgins! and at your feet I seek for refuge and protection. O you who have borne the glorious title of father of Jesus! reject not my humble prayer, but hear it faithfully, and present it for me to Him who disdained not to be called your son, and who will not refuse your petition. Amen.

RESOLUTIONS

DURING the course of the day recall to mind the preceding reflections.

Repeat from time to time the invocation: *St. Joseph, model of purity, pray for us.*

Say three *Hail Marys* daily, to preserve the virtue of purity.

Say the *Our Father* and *Hail Mary* once, and *St. Joseph, pray for us*, three times.

St. Joseph, Model of Attention in Prayer

✣

Sancte Joseph, vir in oratione assidue, ora pro nobis.

St. Joseph, model of attention in prayer,
pray for us.

FIRST POINT: *Necessity of prayer.* We have said that prayer is absolutely necessary to preserve in us the sweet and delicate virtue of purity. It is important frequently to recall to our minds that prayer is essential to the practice of all the virtues, to the avoidance of sin, and in general to the fulfilment of our duties. Prayer is necessary not only as a means of soliciting the graces needed for our souls, but also as an homage of gratitude, adoration, and love towards God, whose infinite bounty, goodness, and love demand this triple return on our part. Our Lord Himself taught us this manner of prayer and left us a most admirable form in the "Our Father." Frequent prayer was recommended in the old law, and we see the exactitude with which the Pharisees observed this counsel; but what they did merely through ceremony St. Joseph, a true Israelite, fulfilled in a spirit of faith, animated by love of God.

SECOND POINT: *Essential qualities of prayer.* Prayer must be accompanied with confidence, humility, and fervor. Prayer is, in itself, an act of humility; for in soliciting favors from God, or when returning thanks for those already received, we find ourselves penetrated with a knowledge of our own unworthiness and misery, and our absolute dependence on God. This humility tends to increase our confidence in the goodness and mercy of God; and prayers uttered with confidence always receive the favor solicited, though for a time it may seem that Almighty God refuses to listen favorably to our petitions. Love, accompanied by fervor, is the third disposition which renders our prayers pleasing to God and efficacious in our advancement in perfection.

"He who ceases to love ceases to pray," says St. Augustine. A few moments' meditation on these words would suffice to convince us of the importance of this most essential quality of prayer.

THIRD POINT: *Prayer in common.* We will find our models in this exercise in the humble cottage at Nazareth. It cannot be deemed rash to assert that Jesus, Mary, and Joseph frequently practised this holy exercise, nor can it be too much to consider Mary and Joseph as being the first to receive from the lips of Jesus that prayer of which He Himself is the author. We are bound, after their example, to establish in our homes, not only the use of this prayer, but also family prayer, at least in the evening; and if this usage has been already established in the family of which we are members, we should endeavor by every means in our power to introduce it into the homes of others. Nor should we content ourselves with merely reciting family prayers, but should, moreover, accustom ourselves to read daily passages from the Scriptures, the "Lives of the Saints," "Imitation of Christ," "History of the Church," or some other work on religion or piety. Incredible advantages have been derived from the observance of these pious practices, not the least of which is the impression which it stamps on the mind of youth. Again, we see how pleasing is this practice to our Lord in the assurance He gives when He says, "Again I say to you that if two of you shall agree upon earth concerning anything whatsoever they shall ask, it shall be done for them by my Father who is in heaven."

PRAYER

HOLY St. Joseph! permit me to unite my prayers with those thou didst offer up with Jesus and Mary. Obtain that I may become more attentive and more devout during prayer. Thou who art in a particular manner patron of family prayer, bless those who unite here on earth in praising Jesus, whose protector thou wert, and obtain for them the graces needed for their salvation. Yes, dear patron, bless them, and bless thy client now imploring thy assistance. Amen.

RESOLUTIONS

DURING the course of the day recall to mind the preceding reflections.

Pray often with confidence, humility, fervor, and love.

Say the *Our Father* and *Hail Mary* once, and *St. Joseph, pray for us*, three times.

ST. JOSEPH, MODEL OF INTERIOR RECOLLECTION

❦

Sancte Joseph, vir in oratione assidue, ora pro nobis.

St. Joseph, most assiduous in prayer,
pray for us.

FIRST POINT: The habit of prayer produces in the soul an interior recollection, which keeps the mind fixed on God, and prevents our being too much absorbed in exterior occupations. One who has acquired this habit lives in the continual presence of the great Being who called him into existence; and, whether employed in laborious duties, or mingling in the busy scenes of life, he never loses sight of that one all-inspiring thought, beside which all earthly joys dwindle into nothingness. This is what we term the interior or meditative life. Let us consider how profound and tranquil must have been the life of St. Joseph, who, whether at work alone or with companions, had his heart and mind centred on God. We behold him ever the same; his noble and serene countenance bearing that indelible mark which the constant union of the soul with God always imprints. Here is our model. Let us endeavor, after his example, to acquire this interior recollection, which will enable us to overcome temptations, whatever be their nature or strength. Habitual prayer is the most effectual means for obtaining this end; and in order to aid those desiring to acquire this practice, we give two forms of prayer.

Second Point: The first form is ejaculatory prayers, which are short aspirations directed to God with all the fervor of which the soul is capable; occupying but a moment, they take from the evil one all power of depriving them of their efficacy. They have, then, a greater influence over the heart of Jesus, forcing Him, as it were, to listen favorably, and grant our petitions. Such, for example, were the aspirations of a Vincent de

Paul, a Teresa, a Francis de Sales, a Magdalen di Pazzi, and many others. What St. Joseph's were we know not; but from a heart so just, so pure, and filled with the love of God as was his heart, aspirations ardent and fervent must have issued. Let us implore St. Joseph to obtain for us that our hearts may be animated with sentiments like unto his.

THIRD POINT: *Mental prayer.* Mental prayer serves to unite our souls to God, and aids in the practice of habitual recollection. On commencing this exercise, we should place ourselves in the presence of God, adore His infinite majesty, acknowledge our own weakness and misery, implore the assistance of the Holy Ghost, and reflect a few moments on the proposed subject. This subject may consist of one of the truths of religion, a good thought, a passage from a pious book, or from the gospel or epistle of the day, a virtue to be acquired, or a vice to be overcome. The reflections made dispose our souls to become worthy recipients of grace; emotions of the heart succeed the reflection, and these, with affections of the will, are the most important parts of the meditation. The exercise is finished by taking a practical resolution for the day, which may be drawn from the subject on which we meditated, or it may be the correction of a predominant fault, or the avoidance of an occasion of sin; and, lastly, an aspiration should be chosen, to be repeated frequently during the day, so that it may serve the twofold duty of recalling to mind the meditation and the resolution taken. St.Francis de Sales, in his " Introduction to a Devout Life," particularly recommends meditation as a means of salvation.

PRAYER

GUARDIAN of Jesus and Mary, I unite my prayers with thy fervent aspirations and holy contemplations. Each day I will place my resolutions under thy protection and that of my Mother Mary, and under this double safeguard I will rest in the full assurance of one day attaining to the sublime height gained by those who applied themselves with zeal and fervor to the constant practice of this holy exercise. Teach me, dear father, to unite my prayers with those of Jesus and Mary, and grant that, after imitating thee closely here on earth, I may one day share in the joy and happiness of thy clients now in heaven. Amen.

RESOLUTIONS

DURING the course of the day recall to mind the preceding reflections.

Repeat from time to time the invocation: *St. Joseph, model of interior recollection, pray for us.*

Learn to become habitually recollected.

Resolve to make a meditation everyday.

Recite today, on your knees, the psalm, "*Miserere.*"

Say the *Our Father* and *Hail Mary* once, and *St. Joseph, pray for us*, three times.

Twenty-eighth Day

St. Joseph, Our Protector

Sancte Joseph, hujus temporis specialis protector, ora pro nobis.

St. Joseph, our present special protector, pray for us.

FIRST POINT: Since the first ages of the Church, the greatest and most illustrious saints and doctors have spoken in highest terms of St. Joseph. Saints Gregory Nazianzen, John Chrysostom, John Damascene, Ambrose, and Augustine were his panegyrists. In the course of centuries, the most eminent men have published his praises. Let it be sufficient for us to name Sts. Bernard, Thomas Aquinas, and Bernardine of Siena. But the honor paid him by the Church has been fully developed since the heresies of Luther and Calvin. St. Teresa seems to have received a special mission from Providence for the promotion of devotion to St. Joseph. Here are her own words relative to this devotion: "I cannot, without wonder, admiration, and love, think of the great graces God has given me through the intercession of St. Joseph, and of the great perils of body and soul from which he has rescued me. It seems that God accords to other saints the power to succor us in certain circumstances, but I know from experience that St. Joseph can help us at all times and on all occasions; as though Jesus Christ wished to demonstrate that, as He was subject to him here on earth, He can now in heaven refuse him nothing. Other persons whom I advised to recommend themselves to his intercession have experienced his power in a similar manner, in consequence of which many now have great devotion to him, and daily feel more and more the truth of what I have asserted."

Second Point: St. Teresa's example has found imitators in every Catholic country, and we find devotion to St. Joseph rapidly increasing. Churches and chapels erected in his honor, religious associations organized under his patronage, congregations placed under his protection, the month of March specially consecrated to his remembrance, the widespread custom of invoking his name after the names of Jesus and Mary—all bear testimony of an especial confidence in the protection of St. Joseph on the part of the children of the Catholic Church; and the Church herself, through those who teach in her name, encourages and supports this generous impulse of confidence and affection. Taking only the pontificate of Pius IX, which is one of the most illustrious and glorious in the long series of popes, we see that almost immediately on his accession to the chair of St. Peter, he established the feast of the "Patronage of St. Joseph." In his memorable address delivered in 1862, he recommended the Church and her wants to the powerful protection of St. Joseph; and later, by his authority, the entire Church was placed under his patronage.

THIRD POINT: The charity of many has become cold; even faith itself is in danger of being lost in many souls; and new means from the treasury of divine Providence are needed to animate zeal, faith, and piety. The wants of the Church have become more pressing since the attacks of modern heresies and the so-called philosophy of rationalism. God gives manifest proofs of the power of St. Joseph and His desire of having him honored and invoked by His children. When friends fail on earth, win for yourselves friends in heaven. What patronage more appropriate than his in our times? At present, all persons seem to desire rank and fortune. Let them picture to their minds the majestic figure of St. Joseph living contented in faith, hope, and charity. The working-classes are pressed down by disguised preachers of pantheism, atheism, and socialism; and secret societies seek to increase their numbers, threatening the world with an overthrow unprecedented in history. Let us invoke this patron of workmen, himself an artisan, whose secret was that of an interior, hidden, humble life entirely devoted to the service of God and the love of his neighbor, in union and company with Jesus and Mary.

PRAYER

REMEMBER, O amiable and powerful protector, St. Joseph! that, according to the testimony of your devoted servant, St. Teresa, no one ever implored your intercession with devotion and confidence without obtaining relief. Animated by this sweet and consoling hope, I come to you, O worthy spouse of the Virgin of virgins! and at your feet I seek for refuge and protection. O you who have borne the glorious title of father of Jesus! reject not my humble prayer, but hear it favorably, and present it for me to Him who disdained not to be called your son, and who will not refuse your petition. Amen.

RESOLUTIONS

DURING the course of the day recall to mind the preceding reflections.

Examine each action, and strive to acquire purity of intention in all you do.

Mortify your desire for drink, in union with the thirst endured by Jesus in His passion.

Twenty-ninth Day

ST. JOSEPH, PATRON OF A HAPPY DEATH

※

Sancte Joseph, protector morientium, ora pro nobis.

Saint Joseph, our protector in the hour of death, pray for us.

THREE reasons are given for the conferring of this title on St. Joseph.

FIRST POINT: *He died in the arms of Jesus and Mary.* To St. Joseph alone among men was given the consoling privilege of dying in the arms of Jesus and Mary. Sweet and tranquil must have been that death, attended as it was by those whose presence can calm the agitated soul, render less painful the final separation of the soul from the body, and alleviate the terrors of the awaiting judgment. Foolish indeed is the man who does not beg for this crowning grace of a happy death. According to a tradition confirmed by revelation, the death of St. Joseph occurred a short time previous to the commencement of the public ministry of our Saviour. Nothing was yet known of the future prodigies to be wrought by Jesus—prodigies which were to reflect so much glory on the poor family of Nazareth. Joseph died obscure and unknown—a perfect type of the Christian death in all its beauty, simplicity, and grandeur. Jesus died on the cross, in torments and sufferings—a victim of propitiation for the sins of men; and Mary, His Mother, expired fifteen years later, consumed with love and the ardent desire of beholding once more her divine Son, with whom she was so intimately united in soul. The death of St. Joseph differed from these two holy deaths, inasmuch as his was accompanied with regret for leaving on earth those who formed his happiness, and who were one day to become the brightest ornaments of heaven. But he died filled with hope in the assurance of a blessed eternity, encouraged by the all-powerful love of Jesus and the sweet words of his Immaculate Spouse. *Moriatur anima mea morte justorum*—"Let my soul die the death of the just." If in my last moments I feel a regret when leaving those I hold dear on earth, and the sorrow of that separation grieve my poor soul, do thou, dear patron, console me in the thought of the glorious reunion of all those united by the ties of blood, friendship, or faith, and whose happiness shall be consummated in heaven.

SECOND POINT: *St. Joseph a powerful mediator with the heart of Jesus.* After Jesus and Mary, what more powerful protector than St. Joseph can we invoke in the solemn and decisive moment on which all depends, when the soul in anguish calls on those who have the power of aiding and protecting her? Gerson says that the prayers addressed by St. Joseph to Jesus and Mary have the force of a command, rather than the form of a supplication. The confidence of a Christian becomes animated and enlivened by these thoughts, and the name of St. Joseph becomes a sure and impenetrable shield against the shafts of hell, and an all-powerful safeguard in the terrors of death.

THIRD POINT: *St. Joseph was taught by Jesus and Mary to adopt us as his children.* No mortal ever obtained so deep a knowledge of the hearts of Jesus and Mary as our dear father, St. Joseph. St. John was called the Beloved, the Apostle of predilection, on account of his having reposed on the bosom of our Saviour; but St. Joseph dwelt with Jesus during thirty years in an intimacy which the angels might have envied, and in the capacity of father. We should often reflect on what we owe St. Joseph in consideration of the numerous graces which he obtained from Jesus for all men, but especially for poor sinners. Moreover, in becoming the adopted father of Jesus, he became ours also; for are we not named, though infinitely unworthy, the brothers of Jesus? Alas! far more appropriate would be the title executioners of the world's Saviour; for we daily become such by the commission of sin. Still, St. Joseph claims us for his children, and the tears and blood of his innocent Son render us dearer in his eyes, while the remembrance of Calvary serves to increase his loving and paternal tenderness towards us. If the affection of a father for his child manifests itself most intensely at the hour of the death of the child, and if, as a Christian, he uses every means in his power to procure for it the graces attendant on a happy death, what, think you, must be the loving, earnest, anxious tenderness of our dear father, St. Joseph, when he sees one of his children on the point of being summoned before a just Judge? With fervor and love he then offers on behalf of the dying one the petitions addressed to himself!

PRAYER

O LOVING father! permit me to address you today as if it were the last day of my life. Inspire me with the sentiments I shall experience on my deathbed; for then my soul will not seek for studied words, but will call on you from the depths of her own weakness and misery, pronouncing your name with love and confidence, and repeating often this little prayer: O dearest Father! whom I have loved so ardently, and so often invoked during life, pray for me now, and obtain for me the grace of a happy death. Amen.

RESOLUTIONS

DURING the course of the day recall to your mind the preceding reflections.

Repeat from time to time: *St. Joseph, patron of a happy death, pray for us.*

Desire death as the only means of consummate union with God.

Recite on your knees the prayers for the faithful departed.

Recite the *Our Father* and *Hail Mary* once, and *St. Joseph, pray for us*, three times.

Thirtieth Day

St. Joseph, Patron of a Happy Death

Sancte Joseph, protector morientium, ora pro nobis.

Saint Joseph, our protector in the hour of death,
pray for us.

LET us again meditate on the important subject that yesterday engaged our attention, and, under the protection of St. Joseph, see what are the means of preparing ourselves for a happy death.

FIRST POINT: *In order to die well, we must confess our sins and receive Holy Communion worthily.* We may say that the best preparation for a happy death is a holy life; also, that a tender devotion to St. Joseph is a great security in one's last moments; and, finally, that all the practices and virtues to which the attention of the faithful has been called during this month, besides aiding them to live in a holy manner, will assist them to die happily. But there is still another means, of which we have not yet spoken, having reserved it for these last days, when the mind would naturally be better prepared to receive it as a truth. These means are Confession and Communion. The most ordinary, and yet the most essential, preparation for a happy death is the worthy reception of the last sacraments. If in our last illness we cannot receive these sacraments, we must endeavor to make up for this loss by our fervent desires and frequent aspirations. We ought daily to pray for the worthy reception of the Holy Viaticum.

SECOND POINT: *We should frequently approach the sacraments of Penance and Holy Eucharist.* Our Holy Mother, the Church, has set apart a specified time, during which we are to confess and communicate under pain of mortal sin. "Confess your sins at least once a year," she says, and adds, "Receive your Creator at Easter." Observe that she says, "at least once a year," manifesting the desire she has of seeing her children approach oftener. The primitive Christians received Holy

Communion every day, or at least as often they assisted at the holy sacrifice. It is indeed a sad sight to see a parish, the members of which seldom or never approach the sacraments; and the first step towards reformation in such should be a change in this particular. It must not be fear that will induce us to receive the body and blood of Jesus Christ; but a loving heart, convinced of its own misery and nothingness, must seek for grace and virtue at the fount of mercy and love. The more frequently and fervently we receive these sacraments during life, the better prepared we will be to receive them at the hour of death. Let us, then, accustom ourselves to frequent Communion.

THIRD POINT: *We should endeavor to prepare ourselves to receive Holy Communion during life with the same dispositions we would wish to have at the hour of death.* Let us adopt this practice in the Communion that is to crown the devotion of this beautiful month of St. Joseph. Let us approach the holy table with deep sentiments of humility, love, hope, and contrition, that our Lord may not only condescend to abide in our hearts, but even desire to enter therein. We may be led to suppose that the thought of receiving our Lord for the last time would fill our hearts with fear and terror; but, on the contrary, it is the Holy Eucharist that makes the thought of death supportable and even sweet, enabling us to meet our Judge without fear, and stand in His august presence as a child before his father. If so much depends on the worthy reception of the sacraments, we ought to be exceedingly circumspect in our preparation, omitting nothing that could in the least degree contribute to make that preparation more devout and pleasing to God. The words used by a holy bishop immediately before his death are applicable to all when receiving the Holy Viaticum: "What need I fear in going to be judged by Him whom I love?"

PRAYER

O GLORIOUS Joseph! my dear patron, inspire me with sentiments of the most ardent love towards Jesus in the Blessed Sacrament; and, as I am about to receive Him at the close of this thy month, prepare, I beseech thee, my poor heart, that it may become an agreeable dwelling for

Him. Grant that, by the worthy reception of this Sacrament during life, I may merit the same grace at the hour of my death. Yes, dear St. Joseph, then more than ever will I need thy assistance. Do not, I implore thee, refuse it; stand near me in that fearful moment; and, when the last struggle is over, accompany me to the judgment-seat, and there, in union with the Blessed Virgin, plead for me until thou obtainest a favorable sentence, that with thee and my Mother Mary I may enjoy God for all eternity. Amen.

RESOLUTIONS

DURING the course of the day recall to mind the preceding reflections.

Repeat from time to time: *St. Joseph, patron of a happy death, pray for us.*

Detach yourself from the goods of earth, and bestow an alms today for that intention.

Bear with the faults of others.

Make some act of mortification in honor of the sufferings of Jesus.

Recite the *Our Father* and *Hail Mary* once, and *St. Joseph, pray for us,* three times.

Thirty-first Day

BENEFITS DERIVED FROM DEVOTION TO ST. JOSEPH

IN closing this month of St. Joseph, we will form the resolution of reciting each day some prayer in his honor. We will endeavor to form the habit of frequently invoking the sweet names of Jesus, Mary, and Joseph, which will serve as ejaculatory prayers, to be repeated during the day and in the hour of temptation, trial, and danger, when everything seems dark around us, and we feel abandoned by God and man. This practice, together with sacrifices offered daily through the merits of Jesus Christ, in union with his blessed Mother and our dear father, St. Joseph, will aid us in keeping the resolutions formed during this month, and serve as incentives to our spiritual progress.

Various examples have been set before us for our encouragement, and from which we are to select those most suitable to our station in life as rules for our future conduct. The author of the "Imitation of Christ" justly observes that "without sacrifice we cannot live the life of love." Our progress in virtue will be according to the violence offered to self. Those souls, then, that are really desirous of advancing in perfection should endeavor to be penetrated with the precious lesson, applicable to every condition of life, and suitable to the acquirement of all Christian virtue. When, at the close of day, we find that we have done nothing for the glory of God, we may justly say with the pagan emperor, Titus, who, regretting that no occasion of pleasing or benefiting others had been given him, exclaimed, "I have lost a day."

Following the example of many devout clients of St. Joseph, let us choose Wednesday in each week as a day on which to render special homage to him, and endeavor to assist at the Holy Sacrifice of the Mass on that day. St. Francis de Sales calls the Mass the sun of spiritual exercises, centre of Christian religion, heart of devotion, soul of piety, and abyss of divine charity, in which God, applying the merits of His precious blood, communicates to us His special graces and favors. If on that day we have not the happiness of making a sacramental Communion, we should at least make a spiritual one, which may be done by ardently desiring to receive our Lord at the moment when the priest and faithful communicate, offering to Him sentiments of humility, respect, and love, imploring the forgiveness of our sins and the grace of being more faithful in future. In fine, during the course of the day, beg St. Joseph to offer all your actions to the Blessed Virgin, and through her to Jesus, that they may be offered by this divine Mediator to His Heavenly Father.

We will strive to be faithful each year to the practices laid down in the month of St. Joseph, and during the month select a few days on which, in retreat, we may review the principal actions of our past life.

ACT OF CONSECRATION TO ST. JOSEPH

I PRESENT myself before thee at the close of these exercises, to consecrate the remainder of my life to thee. Accept, I beseech thee, this poor offering, and, in union with thy immaculate Spouse, present it to Jesus, thy divine Son, by Him to be offered to His Heavenly Father, to receive the smile of approbation and the grace of final perseverance. I consecrate to thee my thoughts, that they may be always subject to reason, and guided by faith. Preserve me from being biased in my opinions by the vain judgments of a wicked, deceitful world. I consecrate to thee my heart, with its emotions, desires, and affections; it needs more restraint than my understanding, on account of its many attractions, preferences, and weaknesses. I consecrate my senses to thee, together with all the actions in which they participate. Grant that, in being organs of the soul, they may be used in procuring the greater honor and glory of God. Instill into my soul a love of virtue which will be the governing principle of all my actions, and guard me by thy grace and love against all the attacks of the evil one. I am surrounded by dangers which threaten to prove my ruin; even the little good I do is so fraught with self-love that it corrupts my best intentions. Overwhelmed with fear at the sight of so many obstacles, I cast myself before thee, imploring thy assistance, and renewing the offerings already made, as also the resolution of doing all for Jesus, in Him and through Him, that, serving Him faithfully in this life, I may enjoy Him for all eternity. Amen.

LITANY OF ST. JOSEPH

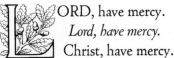ORD, have mercy.
Lord, have mercy.
Christ, have mercy.
Christ, have mercy.
Lord, have mercy.
Lord, have mercy.
Christ, hear us.
Christ, graciously hear us.
God, the Father of Heaven,
Have mercy on us.
God the Son, Redeemer of the world,
Have mercy on us.
God the Holy Ghost,
Have mercy on us.
Holy Trinity, one God,
Have mercy on us.

Holy Mary, Spouse of Joseph,

Holy Joseph, Spouse of the Virgin Mary,

Nursing-father of Jesus,

Man according to God's own heart,

Faithful and prudent servant,

Guardian of the virginity of Mary,

Companion and solace of Mary,

Most pure in virginity,

Most profound in humility,

Most fervent in charity,

Most exalted in contemplation,

Who wast declared to be a just man by the testimony of the Holy Ghost Himself,

Who wast enlightened above all in heavenly mysteries,

Who wast the chosen minister of the counsels of the Most High,

Who wast taught from above the mystery of the Incarnate Word,

Who didst journey to Bethlehem with Mary, thy spouse,

Pray for us.

Who, finding no place in the inn, didst betake thyself to a stable,

Who wast thought worthy to be present when Christ was born and laid in a manger,

Who didst bear in thine arms the Son of God,

Who didst receive the blood of Jesus at His circumcision,

Who didst present Him to His Father in the temple, with Mary, His Mother,

Who, at the warning of the angel, didst fly into Egypt with the child and His Mother,

Who, when Herod was dead, didst return with them into the land of Israel,

Who for three days, with Mary, His Mother, didst seek sorrowing the child Jesus when He was lost at Jerusalem,

Who, after three days, didst with joy find Him sitting in the midst of the doctors,

Who hadst the Lord of lords subject to thee on the earth,

Who wast the happy witness of His hidden life and sacred words,

Pray for us.

Who didst die in the arms of Jesus and Mary,

Whose praise is in the Gospel: The spouse of Mary, of whom was born Jesus,

Humble imitator of the Incarnate Word,

Powerful support of the Church,

Pray for us.

Our advocate, St. Joseph, *hear us.*

Our patron, St. Joseph, *graciously hear us.*

In all our necessities,

In all our distresses,

In the hour of death,

Through thy most chaste espousals,

Through thy paternal care and fidelity,

Through thy love of Jesus and Mary,

Through thy labors and toils,

Through all thy virtues,

Through thy exalted honor and eternal blessedness,

St. Joseph, help us.

Through thy faithful intercession, we, thy clients, beseech thee, *hear us.*

That thou wouldst vouchsafe to obtain for us from Jesus the pardon of our sin,

That thou wouldst vouchsafe to commend us faithfully to Jesus and Mary,

That thou wouldst vouchsafe to obtain for all, both virgins and married, the chastity belonging to their state,

That thou wouldst vouchsafe to obtain for all congregations perfect love and concord,

That thou wouldst vouchsafe to direct all rulers and prelates in the government of their subjects,

That thou wouldst vouchsafe to assist all parents in the Christian education of their children,

That thou wouldst vouchsafe to protect all those that rely upon thy patronage,

That thou wouldst vouchsafe to support, with thy paternal help, all congregations instituted under thy name and patronage,

That thou wouldst vouchsafe to visit and stand by us with Jesus and Mary in the last moment of our life,

We beseech thee, hear us.

That thou wouldst vouchsafe to succor, by thy prayers and intercession, all the faithful departed,

O chaste spouse of Mary,

O faithful nursing-father of Jesus,

Holy Joseph,

We beseech thee, hear us.

Lamb of God, who takest away the sins of the world, *spare us, O Lord,*

Lamb of God, who takest away the sins of the world, *graciously hear us, O Lord.*

Lamb of God, who takest away the sins of the world, *have mercy on us.*

Christ, hear us.
  Christ, graciously hear us.

Pray for us, O blessed Joseph!
  That we may be made worthy of the promises of Christ.

LET US PRAY:

O GOD! who didst choose St. Joseph to be the spouse of Blessed Mary, ever virgin, and to be the guardian and foster-father of Thy beloved Son, our Lord Jesus Christ, we humbly beseech Thee to grant us, through his patronage and merits, such purity of mind and body that, being clean from every stain and clothed with the true marriage-garment, we may, by Thy great mercy, be admitted to the heavenly nuptials: through the same Jesus Christ, our Lord. Amen.

O God! who in thine ineffable providence didst vouchsafe to choose blessed Joseph to be the spouse of Thy most holy Mother, grant, we beseech Thee, that we may be made worthy to receive him for our intercessor in heaven whom on earth we venerate as our holy protector: who livest and reignest, world without end. Amen.

Guardian of virgins and father, holy Joseph, to whose faithful custody Christ Jesus, very Innocence, and Mary, Virgin of virgins, were committed, I pray and beg of thee by these dear pledges, Jesus and Mary, free me from all uncleanness, and make me, with spotless mind, pure heart, and chaste body ever most chastely to serve Jesus and Mary all the days of my life. Amen.

Prayer to St. Joseph

To Obtain the Spirit of our Vocation

GLORIOUS St. Joseph! chaste spouse of Mary, our good Mother, and nursing-father of Jesus, our amiable Saviour; humbly prostrate at your feet, we choose you anew for our good father, and beg you to receive us among the members of your privileged children.

We thank you with our whole heart for having given us a place in this holy family, of which you are the protector as the father. Burning with the desire of responding worthily to our holy vocation, we conjure you, with the most filial confidence, to obtain for us its spirit and virtues. Yes, great saint, grant that, following your example, we may every day make new progress in humility, obedience, recollection, the spirit of poverty, and, above all, in the love of Jesus and Mary.

May we, like you, find our delight in serving this sweet Jesus in the person of His suffering members, as you had the happiness of serving Him in His own person. Deign to crown all your favors by obtaining for us the grace to die like you in the arms of Jesus and Mary, that we may go to share your happiness in the company of our beloved sisters and brothers who have gone before us, and who await us near you in the heavenly country. Amen.

Novena to St. Joseph

Directions for Each Day of the Novena:

Begin with the Litany of the Saints, say one of the following prayers, then recite the *Our Father* and the *Hail Mary* three times, and conclude with the Oblation: *O holy Joseph!* etc., found at the end of the Novena.

First Day

✠

BLESSED St. Joseph! born to be the guardian of Jesus, the protector and consoler of Mary, make powerful intercession for me, that my pious resolutions may not prove abortive, that I may be born to an interior and spiritual life, that I may have such an increase of sanctity, so ardent a love of purity, so great a conviction of my own vileness, so clear a light of the emptiness and vanity of worldly grandeur, as to esteem and relish only things that are eternal.

Through our Lord Jesus Christ. Amen.

SECOND DAY

❧

OMNIPOTENT Creator! whose unerring providence adds joy every moment to the angels in heaven and to the saints upon earth, I most humbly beg, through the intercession of St. Joseph, that I may cheerfully acquiesce and rejoice in everything that comes from Thy fatherly hand; that I may be vigorous in executing Thy divine will, and glorify Thee in my present state. Grant me the true spirit of mortification to subdue my stubborn passions, to satisfy for what is past, and to be a preservation from future dangers. Grant that, by purity of intention, the meanest of my actions may be acceptable to Thee, as was the mite of the poor woman which was put into the treasury of the temple.

Through Jesus Christ our Lord. Amen.

THIRD DAY

OMNIPOTENT God! at whose command every tree produces fruit of its kind, grant, through the intercession of Mary and Joseph, that I may serve Thee faithfully in the state in which Thou hast placed me. I firmly believe all Thou hast revealed; protect me, lest I should be found among the number of those foolish virgins who carried lamps without oil. Assist me with Thy powerful grace, that I may be humble, charitable, and chaste, and not be like the barren fig-tree, fit only to become fuel for eternal flames. This grace I implore through the infinite merits of Jesus, my Saviour. Amen.

FOURTH DAY

✦

HOLY GHOST! God of all comfort! if Thou seest it expedient for the security of my salvation that I should be oppressed with tribulation, permit me not to fall. Infinite power! bear me up; Thou knowest my weakness. Favor me with grace, that I may be compassionate towards my neighbor, and govern myself with the same spirit of lenity and charity as if the case were my own. I deplore my censorious temper, and resolve to be upon my guard. I return Thee thanks for inspiring me with the resolution of becoming better; but of myself, I am not able to persevere in my good intentions. I beg Thy assistance, that I may fulfill what Thou commandest; and then, dear Lord, command what Thou pleasest. Afflict me with such crosses as I can endure, that I may discharge at least a part of the great debt due to the divine justice. Grant, through the intercession of St. Joseph, that after my temporal trials, whether exterior or interior, I may find that permanent joy with which Thou renderest him and his Immaculate Spouse eternally happy. Through the merits of our Lord Jesus Christ. Amen.

FIFTH DAY

INFINITE God! how truly may it be said of me, The ox knoweth his owner, and the ass his master's crib, but thou knowest not thy Lord! I admire thy love and charity. I am ashamed of my tepidity and ingratitude. Infinite Goodness! I come too late to love Thee; but although it be the eleventh hour, bestow on me the promised reward; be to me a Saviour. Thou who hast bled for me, let me partake of Thy eternal charity. Grant that through the intercession of St. Joseph, my good resolutions may be perfected. I also beg that when I entertain Thee in the most blessed Sacrament, I may be favored with the same sentiments of adoration, love, and thanksgiving that St. Joseph experienced when received from Simeon to restore Thee to Thy blessed Mother. Amen.

Sixth Day

JESUS, my Maker and my Master, without whose merciful assistance I walk in darkness and perish! I most humbly beg, through the intercession of St. Joseph, that Thou wilt grant me grace to escape from the servitude of sin, under which I have so long groaned, in order that I may enjoy the liberty of Thy faithful servants. I have frequently experienced Thy goodness, and I know Thy power; my trust is in both. Oh! grant me constancy to despise the allurements of the world, and to remain undaunted under afflicting terrors. My dear Redeemer, I have too often lost Thee by sin: I have willingly and wilfully parted with Thee to follow my corrupt inclinations. O God! who didst come to seek sinners, take pity on me, who am the greatest. Thou art now pleased to bless me with such a true sense of my former offences that I grieve not so much for the fear of punishment as for the misfortune of having offended Thee, the centre of all goodness.

I steadfastly purpose, through Thy grace, to seek Thee seriously by the reformation of my life, that I may find Thee in the heavenly Jerusalem reigning with the Father and the Holy Ghost, world without end. Amen.

SEVENTH DAY

OMNIPOTENT God! who descended from heaven to bring fire on earth, inflame my frozen heart, that I may imitate the virtues of St. Joseph. As a poor wretch at the gate of some noble and generous prince, expecting an alms, so I appear before Thee, wounded in all my senses by sin, and imploring charity in my great distress. I grieve for what is passed, not because I fear, but because I love. Nothing has succeeded with me, because I never consulted Thee as I ought. I hope, O Lord! that I do not come too late. I beg, through the intercession of St. Joseph, that I may avoid evil and do good; that I may leave the broad road of iniquity, and walk in the narrow road that leads to eternal happiness; that I may consecrate the remaining days of my short life to Thy honor, and attain the end for which I was created—to admire, praise, and love Thee for ever and ever. Amen.

EIGHTH DAY

✿

MOST glorious patriarch, my dear patron! Blessed are the eyes that see what you now see. Through the infinite merits of Christ, and by your powerful intercession, I hope, with holy Job, that in my flesh I shall see God my Saviour. Stretch out, in favor of your unworthy client, those happy arms that so often bore the Son of God and provided for Him. Petition that I may live, as I wish to die, always in the divine favor. I humbly implore you to entreat your Immaculate Spouse to unite her supplications with yours, that I may be of the blessed number of the elect. I most sincerely desire that you may be present at the dreadful hour of my death, and that the last words uttered by my parting breath may be Jesus, Mary, and Joseph.

Thy mercy is above all thy works. O most holy Trinity! I now appeal from the tribunal of Thy justice, and prostrate myself before the throne of Thy mercy, to obtain the pardon of my sins, and grace to persevere in keeping Thy commandments to the end of my life. Who livest and reignest one God for ever and ever. Amen.

Ninth Day

❦

HOLY St. Joseph! you who are that good and faithful servant to whom God committed the care of his family; whom he appointed guardian and protector of the life of Jesus Christ, the comfort and support of his holy Mother, and the depositary of his great design of the redemption of mankind; you who had the happiness of living with Jesus and Mary, and of dying in their arms; chaste spouse of the Mother of God, model and patron of pure souls, humble, patient, and reserved, be moved with the confidence we place in your intercession, and accept with kindness this testimony of our devotion.

We give thanks to God for the signal favor he hath been pleased to confer on you, and we conjure him, through your intercession, to enable us to imitate your virtues. Pray for us, then, O great saint! and by that love which you had for Jesus and Mary, and by the love which they had for you, obtain for us the incomparable happiness of living and dying in the love of Jesus and Mary. Amen.

A VOTIVE OBLATION TO ST. JOSEPH

TO CHOOSE HIM FOR OUR PATRON

HOLY Joseph! virgin spouse of the Virgin Mother of God, most glorious advocate of all such as are in danger or in their last agony, and most faithful protector of all the servants of Mary, your dearest Spouse, I, *(state your name)*, in the presence of Jesus and Mary, do, from this moment, choose you for my powerful patron and advocate, in order that I may obtain the grace of a most happy death; I firmly resolve and purpose never to forsake you, nor to say or do anything against your honor. Receive me, therefore, for your constant servant, and recommend me to the constant protection of Mary, your dearest Spouse, and to the everlasting mercies of Jesus, my Saviour. Assist me in all the actions of my life; I now offer them to the greater and everlasting glory of Jesus and Mary, as well as to your own. Amen.

Thirty Days' Prayer to Saint Joseph

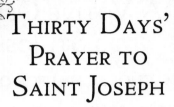

Chaste Spouse of the ever Immaculate and Blessed Virgin Mary, and reputed Father of Jesus Christ.

❧

To Obtain a Happy Death, and other Good Intentions

EVER blessed and glorious Joseph, kind and indulgent father, and compassionate friend of all in sorrow, through that bitter grief with which thy heart was saturated when thou didst behold the sufferings of the Infant Saviour, and in prophetic view didst contemplate His most ignominious passion and death, take pity, I beseech thee, in my poverty and necessities; counsel me in my doubts, and console me in all my anxieties. Thou art the good father and protector of orphans, the advocate of the defenceless, the patron of those who are in need and desolation. Do not, then, disregard the petition of thy poor child; my sins have drawn down upon me the just displeasure of my God, and hence I am surrounded with sorrows. To thee, O amiable guardian of the poor neglected family of Nazareth! do I fly for shelter and protection. Listen, then, I entreat of thee, with a father's solicitude, to the earnest prayer of thy poor supplicant, and obtain for me the objects of my petition. I ask it by the infinite mercy of the eternal Son of God, which induced Him to assume our nature, and be born into this world of sorrow. I ask it by the grief which filled thy heart when, ignorant of the mystery wrought in thy Immaculate Spouse, thou didst fear thou shouldst be separated from her.

I ask it by that weariness, solicitude, and suffering which thou didst endure when thou soughtest in vain at the inns of Bethlehem a shelter for the sacred Virgin and a birth-place for the Infant God, and when, being everywhere refused, thou wert obliged to consent that the Queen of Heaven should give birth to the world's Redeemer in a wretched stable. I ask it by that most sad and painful duty imposed on thee when, the divine Child being eight days old, thou wert obliged to inflict a deep wound on His tender body, and thus be the first to make flow that sacred blood which was to wash away the sins of the world. I ask it by the sweetness and power of that sacred name, Jesus, which thou didst confer on the adorable Infant. I ask it by that mortal anguish inflicted on thee by the prophecy of holy Simeon, which declared the child Jesus and his holy Mother the future victims of their love and our sins. I ask it through that sorrow and anguish which filled thy soul when the angel declared to thee that the life of the child Jesus was sought by His enemies, from whose impious designs thou wert obliged to fly with Him and His blessed Mother into Egypt. I ask it by all the pains, fatigues, and toils of that long and perilous pilgrimage. I ask it by all the sorrows thou didst endure when in Egypt thou wert not able, even by the sweat of thy brow, to procure poor food and clothing for thy most poor family. I ask it by all the grief thou didst feel each time the divine Child asked for a morsel of bread, and thou hadst it not to give Him. I ask it by all thy solicitude to preserve the sacred Child and the Immaculate Mary during thy second journey, when thou wert ordered to return to thy native country. I ask it by thy peaceful dwelling in Nazareth, in which so many joys and sorrows were mingled. I ask it by thy extreme affliction in being three days deprived of the company of the adorable Child. I ask it by thy joy at finding Him in the Temple, and by the ineffable consolation imparted to thee in the cottage of Nazareth with the company and society of the little Jesus. I ask it by that wonderful condescension by which He subjected Himself to thy will. I ask it through that dolorous view, continually in thy mind, of all thy Jesus was to suffer. I ask it by that painful contemplation which made thee foresee the divine little hands and feet, now so active in serving thee, one day to be pierced with cruel nails; that head, which rested gently on thy bosom, crowned with sharp thorns; that delicate body, which thou didst tenderly fold in thy mantle and press to thy heart, stripped and extended on a cross. I ask it by that heroic sacrifice of thy will and best affections, by which thou didst offer up to the Eternal Father the last awful moment when the Man-God was to expire for our salvation. I ask it by that perfect love and conformity with which thou didst receive the divine order to depart from this life and from the company of Jesus and Mary. I ask it by that exceeding great joy which filled thy soul when the Redeemer of the world, triumphant over death and hell, entered into the possession of His kingdom, and conducted thee also into it with especial honors. I ask it through

Mary's glorious assumption, and through that interminable bliss which with her thou wilt eternally derive from the presence of God. O good father! I beseech thee, by all thy sufferings, sorrows, and joys, to hear me, and to obtain the grant of my earnest petitions. (*Here name them or reflect on them.*) Obtain for all those who have asked thy prayers all that is useful to them in the designs of God. And finally, my dear protector, be thou with me and all who are dear to me in our last moments, that we may eternally chant the praises of

JESUS, MARY, AND JOSEPH.

Amen.

Additional titles available from

St. Augustine Academy Press
Books for the Traditional Catholic

Titles by Mother Mary Loyola:

Blessed are they that Mourn
Confession and Communion
Coram Sanctissimo (Before the Most Holy)
First Communion
First Confession
Forgive us our Trespasses
Hail! Full of Grace
Heavenwards
Holy Mass/How to Help the Sick and Dying
Home for Good
Jesus of Nazareth: The Story of His Life Written for Children
The Child of God: What comes of our Baptism
The Children's Charter
The Little Children's Prayer Book
The Soldier of Christ: Talks before Confirmation
Welcome! Holy Communion Before and After

Titles by Father Lasance:

The Catholic Girl's Guide
The Young Man's Guide

Tales of the Saints:

A Child's Book of Saints by William Canton
A Child's Book of Warriors by William Canton
Illustrated Life of the Blessed Virgin by Rev. B. Rohner, O.S.B.
Legends & Stories of Italy by Amy Steedman
Mary, Help of Christians by Rev. Bonaventure Hammer
The Book of Saints and Heroes by Lenora Lang
Saint Patrick: Apostle of Ireland
The Story of St. Elizabeth of Hungary by William Canton

Check our Website for more:
www.staugustineacademypress.com

CPSIA information can be obtained
at www.ICGtesting.com
Printed in the USA
LVHW080451050122
707782LV00002BA/7